DIE YOUNG

HAYLEY
DIMARCO

DIE
YOUNG

DIE YOUNG

DIE YOUNG

DIE

MICHAEL
DIMARCO

BURYING YOUR SELF
IN CHRIST

:: CROSSWAY

WHEATON, ILLINOIS

Library of Congress Cataloging-in-Publication Data
DiMarco, Hayley.
   Die young : burying your self in Christ / Hayley DiMarco and Michael DiMarco.
     p. cm.
   ISBN 978-1-4335-3057-9 (tp)
    1. Christian life. 2. Self-denial. I. DiMarco, Michael. II. Title.
   BV4647.S4D56   2012
   248.4—dc23   2011026424

CONTENTS

A NOTE TO THE READER

To better serve you, we've created supplemental video content to coincide with every chapter in this book. These brief videos from Michael and Hayley are less than five minutes in length and are useful for group studies and individual reflection. Check them out online at: www.crossway.org/dieyoung.

Sincerely,
THE CROSSWAY TEAM

PROLOGUE

Lord, hast Thou declared that no
man shall see Thy face and live?
Then let me die, that I may see Thee.
AUGUSTINE

HERE LIES
HAYLEY

At the moment that I died my life changed forever. It was a slow, painful death—one that I didn't see coming but felt with a persistent, gnawing pain—kind of like undiagnosed cancer. Sure I felt yucky, I was tired, worn out, and exasperated, but I didn't see death coming. But when it came, boy, did my life change. Suddenly I could see more clearly. I could understand things I couldn't understand before. All my fear, worry, doubt, and even stress were all gone. I was finally at peace, finally dead to this world and living for Christ.

I'm not talking about my physical death here; that hasn't come yet, and I expect it to be even better than this, but I'm talking about the death to self that I experienced not long ago and can't quit returning to. *Die Young* is about that kind of death, the dying-to-self kind of death, the "living sacrifice" that Paul wrote about to the Romans in Romans 12. This ability to deny yourself so that you don't serve your desires over his—this is what dying young is all about.

HERE LIES
MICHAEL

The majority of my life has been me living for me. Even when I identified myself as a Christian, it was about the social aspects of my life or the fire insurance involved. My faith was all about keeping me alive and keeping Christ buried. It's like Freddy Krueger or some other horror movie villain; every time you think I'm dead, my hand comes up out of the ground to dig my way out of the grave, looking to resume living my life on my terms (and usually to a grisly end).

My die young moment came when I started focusing on Jesus's two great commands: love God with my all, plus love others, even the unlovable, as much as I love myself. This second command was masterful because Jesus knows just how capable we are of loving ourselves and how that's not something that we need to be taught. Jesus didn't say "love yourself so you can love others." So to die young for me was to remove me as the center of my world and to put God and others in my place—loving and serving them as much, if not more, than I do myself.

"If I only knew then what I know now" is something everyone who has done any degree of living can say. Why must it take us so long to learn, so long to die? If we could only trust God and die young, die to our lusts, our idols, our obsessions, then we could see the fruit of that death so much earlier and find great gain. But when we put off the death that leads to life, we live with regret. Regret is a sad thing; it speaks of a life of mistakes, of failures, and of sin. But regret can be a thing of the past. It no longer has to be your condition, because today, no matter how old you are, you can die young. In fact, you are never too old to die young. If you think that you are, then you're continuing to do what you've always done and assuming somehow things are going to change. Brilliant!

God wants you to die young today. He wants you to take up your cross and follow him. He wants you to deny yourself, to say no to the promptings of your flesh and of this world and yes to the promptings of his Spirit. To die young is to do all those things. It is to give up your right to yourself so that no one can be your master but God himself. A life that refuses to die to self is a life that refuses the very words of God: *"Then Jesus told his disciples, 'If anyone would come after me, let him deny himself and take up his cross and follow me. For whoever would save his life will lose it, but whoever loses his life for my sake will find it. For what will it profit a man if he gains the whole world and forfeits his soul?'"* (Matt. 16:24–26).

TO DIE YOUNG
IS TO LIVE

When God calls a man, he bids him come and die.
DIETRICH BONHOEFFER

Identification with the death of Jesus Christ means identification with Him to the death of everything that never was in Him.
OSWALD CHAMBERS

T o die young is to live for Christ and nothing else, to be set free from the bondage of sin and self, and to live a new kind of life. Those who die young are emotionally bulletproof (or close to it), because they have already died to everything in them that another person could damage or break. In the 1800s, missionary James Calvert left for the Fiji Islands to share Jesus with the cannibals living there. The captain of the ship that brought him tried to dissuade his going by saying,

"You will lose your life and the lives of those with you if you go among such savages." To which Calvert replied, *"We died before we came here!"*[1]

Jim Calvert knew what it was to die young, and because of that he could do what other men were too afraid to do. His confidence was built on the fact that he had already given his life away, so no one else could harm him. His life, and the lives of those like him, are a shining example of the beauty of the death and burial of self.

When you die young, you give all of your needs, fears, worries, wants, hopes, dreams, and failures over to the One who can handle them. And you learn now, while your youth is fresh and your days are bright (if you've got any days left at all), to start living like you mean it—to live out of the center of your faith, giving up your rights and your demands so that his will is all you see. When you live a life bent on dying to yourself and living for the Father, you live a life of purpose and passion, a life of hope and peace, and nothing can ever shake you or break you that isn't the very hand of God himself molding you and shaping you into his own precious image.

When you die young you bury yourself fully in Christ. It's the stuff of horror movies to be buried alive—scratching and clawing at the casket lid, gasping for air. "Buried" and "alive" do not go well together. The only good buried person is a dead one. So when we speak of burying yourself in Christ, we are talking about your "self" death. To remain fully devoted to your self-interests, your self-respect, your self-importance, and your selfishness is to remain alive in yourself and to serve yourself. But when you die young, you are able to bury yourself and live in Christ.

Think about it like this: When a man buries himself in his work, he puts all his energy into it and has little left for anything else. People bury themselves in things they hope will save them, but the only one who can truly be saved is the one who is buried in Christ. That is the gospel—the saving truth that Christ's love was so compelling, so complete that he would give his own life for yours that you might have eternal life with him.

God wants you to die young. He wants you to die today to those things that promise to set you free but really keep you in bondage. He wants you to die to that obsessive need to please yourself, to comfort yourself, and to enjoy yourself so that you can live only to please him. The idea of dying young is not an easy one. In fact, when the world thinks of dying young, they think of tragedy, of a life that was cut too short—and they are right. But dying young isn't about ending your physical life but rather your self-life, and in that process discovering a more real life than you had ever imagined. Jesus promises an abundant life to all who turn from themselves and bury themselves in him (John 10:10). And that can be yours today if only you are willing to die young.

So as you work your way through this book, consider the idea that the life of faith is going to change you—because that's what it must do. Many have said it, and let us join the crowd, "If God isn't changing you, then he hasn't saved you." Let God start changing you today. Don't let the status quo be acceptable to you; want more of what Jesus has to give, and let your life change today so that you may die young and live your life for Jesus.

CHAPTER 1

DEATH
IS THE NEW
LIFE

Whoever finds his life will lose it, and whoever loses his life for my sake will find it.

MATTHEW 10:39

God's will is sweetest to us, when it triumphs at our cost.

FABER

L ife is good. Who doesn't want more life? The end of life is something no one wants to think about and something everyone wants to avoid. The fountain of youth, should it exist, would be the busiest water feature in the world if it could truly make us live forever. Human beings want to live; they don't want to die. Death is a permanent end to life as we know it and often comes after excruciating pain.

Losing your life tears you out of your body and your world, and that idea can scare even the bravest of souls. Death is ugly. It weakens our bodies and sucks out our energy. The deathbed is a sad and tragic place for those who love the dying. And so death is something we all want to avoid as long as possible.

Incredibly, in the beginning when God created the first parents, he gave them their own source of youth in the garden. It was the Tree of Life. And they could eat from it anytime they wanted. And the fruit they ate gave them what the name suggests—life without death. Paradise. They had no fear of an end because there was no end in sight. But when Adam and Eve wanted more than just life, through the knowledge of good and evil that the tree by the same name offered, they ate of the forbidden fruit, and their sin led to death for us all.

Romans 5:17 confirms that death when it says, "Because of one man's trespass [Adam], death reigned through that one man." And the result has been the decay of humanity ever since. In fact, as soon as humans stop growing, they start dying.

Now because of this series of events seen in the life of man, we now know the result of sin to be death (Rom. 6:23). Death takes over when sin gives it access to the life of the sinner. Sin starts the decaying process. Sin, while it seemingly offers immediate and great reward, ultimately puts the sinner into a bondage that weakens and eventually destroys.

HIS DEATH IS YOUR LIFE

But that's not the end of the story. Just as one man's sin led to death for all mankind, so one man's death led to life for all of mankind (Rom. 5:19). In a weird twist of events, death becomes life in one fell swoop, when by dying on that cross Jesus redeemed us all from the bondage of sin and death. It goes like this: *"Do you not know that all of us who have been baptized into Christ Jesus were baptized into his death? We were buried therefore with him by baptism into death, in order that, just as Christ was raised from the dead by the glory of the Father, we too might walk in newness of life"* (Rom. 6:3–4). And there it is—death is the new life.

See, God offered the death of his Son on the cross in order to remove the power of death from you and to give you a new life, one free from the wages of sin. In this new life you are set free from the bondage of the world that so easily threatens to destroy you. Through death, the death of Jesus, you can say with Paul: *"The world has*

HERE LIES
HAYLEY

It's not that I fear death itself but the pain that leads up to it. And I am certain that in the area of natural disaster, pain is going to take over my life, and that's why I'm naturally scared of flying and of tornadoes, hurricanes, and earthquakes. These catastrophic events scare me to death. I love the thought of heaven and I can understand the glory of that life, but the road to death is a scary one. And so my instinct is to obsess over potential disaster, and I naturally panic when that potential looms. So any thought of death isn't something that comes naturally or effortlessly to me, but something that I've had to learn to embrace over time and through faith.

been crucified to me, and I to the world" (Gal. 6:15). When the world no longer holds the power to harm or control you because you have died to it, you are set free and a new life is the result.

His death, then, allows for your death. As it says in 2 Corinthians 5:14–15, *"One has died for all, therefore all have died; and he died for all, that those who live might no longer live for themselves but for him who for their sake died and was raised."*

His death is the one and only thing that allows you to no longer live for yourself. This movement from death to life isn't one of human strength or ingenuity but of cross and blood, of Father and Son, of power and might.

In Galatians 2:19–21 this idea takes form in the words, *"For through the law I died to the law, so that I might live to God. I have been crucified with Christ. It is no longer I who live, but Christ who lives in me. And the life I now live in the flesh I live by faith in the Son of God, who loved me and gave himself for me. I do not nullify the grace of God, for if righteousness were through the law, then Christ died for no purpose."* If righteousness, or the death we are talking about, was through the law, then Christ died for no purpose. Those are some powerful words.

No one who believes in the saving work of the cross would dare say that Christ's death was pointless. But that is what we do when we work toward salvation or death in our own power, when we respond to the pangs of guilt that tell us we are too bad to be good, too selfish to die young. Those are the lies of the Devil and need to be treated as such. In your own strength you can do none of this. Dying to self is too powerful, too supernatural for a person to do without the power of someone who is greater. But through the power of the Holy Spirit in you, this death is attainable. Up to this point, if you haven't walked away from yourself, if you are feeling over-whelmed with the whole idea, then take heart. That is as it should be; you cannot do this on your own—and thank God, because if you could, then he wouldn't be God at all, but a mere accessory to your spiritual life. God is essen-tial to all your life, especially your death life.

YOUR SELF DEATH

So death becomes, for the believer, a valuable concept, both in the Savior's death and our own. The Savior's death is crucial in the life of faith. Without the death, burial, and resurrection of Christ there isn't a Christian. His death is your life. But what about your own death? How does dying young affect the lives of believers, and why is this concept the focus of a book? While it sounds counterintuitive to many, let's see how biblically intuitive it is, *"For If you live according to the flesh you will die, but if by the Spirit you put to death the deeds of the body, you will live"* (Rom. 8:13).

See the correlation? Those who live according to the flesh—self—will die. But, those who live by the Spirit of God put self to death and thus live. Death becomes life for the believer who makes life a living sacrifice by refus-ing to serve, or live for, the flesh with all its "needs," complaints, wants, and desires.

Jesus explains it to us this way: *"If anyone would come after me, let him deny himself and take up his cross daily and follow me. For whoever would save his life will lose it, but whoever loses his life for my sake will save it.*

For what does it profit a man if he gains the whole world and loses or forfeits himself?" (Luke 9:23–25).

Talk about backward. Lose your life by denying yourself daily, and then and only then can you find it? Fight to save your self-life and you end up miserable and losing it? Huh? But this is the paradox of faith. Death is the new life.

Death is painful. It's invasive and ultimately dangerous. Death threatens a part of you, if not all of you. And it brings suffering and struggle along with it. But when you can see that the death of self in you results in life, you can be set free to suffer and to suffer well. In fact, all the suffering that you face at the hands of your self-death is the suffering of progress (some might say sanctification). It's like the weight lifter, whose muscles pull and tear, whose body aches and throbs at the end of the day, who doesn't suffer from the resentment of pain but the welcome of it, knowing that pain is doing its work. The weightlifter looks beyond the painful muscles to the goal of the pain—growth—and because of that the suffering is welcomed. Welcomed suffering, with a clear goal of growth, is somehow less difficult to endure than unwelcome or purposeless suffering.

In this world you will face suffering, there is no question, but it's what you do with your suffering and pain that matters. **To suffer and to refuse to let the suffering destroy in you that which separates you from God is to waste your suffering and even prolong it.** Suffering has a very important role in the life of man. **In matters of the spirit suffering teaches us more than happiness ever could.** And nowhere is the value of suffering and trials given more explanation than in James 1:2–4 where we are told to *"count it all joy, my brothers, when you meet trials of various kinds, for you know that the testing of your faith produces steadfastness. And let steadfastness have its full effect, that you may be perfect and complete, lacking in nothing."*

The trials and suffering of your life offer you the opportunity to die, and sometimes they make you want to die. But suffering is senseless, and so is the pain that goes along with it, if it serves no other purpose than to destroy you. Here's the rub: it must destroy something, and it's your choice what that will be. Will suffering destroy your hope and your faith, leaving you with nothing solid to stand on, alone and empty, or will your suffering destroy the parts of you that tie you to the things of this earth and keep your focus off the God of heaven?

If you believe that death is the new life, then you have to know that you will face trials, you will suffer; but those trials and suffering, now mean something, having a value placed on them, and so will become significantly easier to handle. In fact, when death is your new life, death loses its sting. And this is important because death will come, but how much suffering it will bring depends on your ideas about death. The apostle Paul thought about this death like this, *"I consider that the sufferings of this present time are not worth comparing with the glory that is to be revealed to us"* (Rom. 8:18).

So suffering, though it is unpleasant and exhausting, is really nothing compared with what is coming. That's the state of mind you have to have when you consider dying young—when you consider putting aside your own wants, likes, preferences, passions, dreams, and desires—all for the will of God. When you say no to the things you used to say yes to, when you accept trials as an important part of the life of faith, and when you know the life that comes from the death they bring to you, then it all becomes easier to bear. If you fear death, then death has a grip on you. Just as fearing another human being tightens his or her grip on you, so death does the same. That's why we look to find perspective about death and life, dying to self and living for self, so that we can be free from the bondage of fear. That bondage is a false one for those who have accepted the death and resurrection of Christ as their salvation, because through his death he would destroy *"the one who has the power of death, that is, the devil, and deliver all those who through fear of death were subject to lifelong slavery"* (Heb. 2:14–15).

The fear of death is a lifelong and unnecessary slavery. What a tragedy, when that slavery has already been broken by the gift of Jesus's death—a death that we are to model when we bury our "selves" in him and experience freedom from fear.

So for the believer your welcomed death becomes your new life of freedom. Now let's consider the life that comes when you die young and embrace the life of Christ in you.

THE LIFE OF THE DEAD

We've established up to this point that life comes out of death. So now let's talk about what kind of life comes out of death. To die young is to be free—free from the bondage to sin, to pain, and even at times, to suffering. But to die young with the goal of attaining anything other than complete abandonment to the Father is not death at all but a return to the self-life. There are changes that come to the soul that abandons itself to the control of the Holy Spirit, and these changes are worth considering; but we list these not so that you will have them in mind when you die young or as your reason to die, but so that you can grab hold of the importance of the death that no longer responds to self but solely to the promptings of the Holy Spirit.

THE LIFE OF CONTENTMENT

Contentment is something everyone craves and we remain discontent until we get it. This is insanity, especially since discontentment is so selfish and depressing. When we are discontent, we look at what we have around us and decide that it isn't what we expected or deserved. It's subpar, and with that assessment we have two unholy responses to choose from: we can either choose to give up or to get going.

To give up is to settle in to the boredom and meaninglessness of life and to accept the fact that we will never get what we want or be who we want to be. In this state, discontentment is the status quo, and as such, it peppers every aspect of our lives. It ultimately leads to feelings of regret, resentment, bitterness, depression, anger, and even fear—all not only uncomfortable feelings but also sinful ones. They are sinful because of what they say about God. If anything you think carries with it the accusation that God messed up, neglected you, is a bad gifter, or is in some way unfaithful to his Word that promises he will never leave you or forsake you, will provide for you, will comfort you, will be everything you need and more, then you are calling him a liar and an unholy God. This carries with it the sting and stench of sin that threatens to destroy not only your faith but also your hope and your peace.

Let's take a look at the other way many respond to their discontentment and that is to choose *to get going*. In this response, the discontented get to work to change their environments, to change their lives in order to get to that which they dreamed, hoped, or imagined would be their lives. Their passion, their directive, their drive is set on achievement, on making something happen. This is the stuff of late-night infomercials. Their focus shifts from the God who makes things happen to themselves who make things happen. And in this subtle shift, self becomes the god who is followed, obeyed, and worshiped.

When you die young, discontentment loses its punch because discontentment requires the elevation of self to a place where more than is given is required, where good enough isn't good enough, and where imperfection is bothersome, if not depressing. But the death of self removes self from the picture and replaces it with the Father. With him on the throne, contentment is the only response, because the life you live isn't bent on pleasing self but on pleasing him. **Pleasing him is easy when it comes to what you have been given, because all it requires is thankfulness and trust that what he has given is the best thing for you.** You can know this because of who he is. His attributes confirm that he is not only perfect in all his ways, but kind, faithful, all-powerful, all-knowing, and love itself. When life doesn't turn out the way you thought, when what you have isn't what you wanted, you can remind yourself that both good and bad come from God (Lam. 3:38). If he has given it to you, then you can be certain that it is for your benefit, if only you will accept it as such and allow it to do the work of removing you from the throne of your life.

The secret is that dying young leads to contentment because it sees life as designed and orchestrated by God himself, meant to perfect those he loves and to draw them away from sin and toward holiness and his perfection. When you die young, circumstances and stuff matter less because self no longer demands to be pleased but to serve the one who pleases (Eccles. 2:26).

THE LIFE OF SANCTIFICATION

Now, let's look at the sanctification that comes with death. The life of faith requires death in order for it to come into existence and then grow. Your salvation required the death of Christ, and your sanctification means the death of the part of you that clings to things that God rejects. Sanctification is the process that begins on the day of conversion through the power of the Holy Spirit (2 Thess. 2:13) and continues for the rest of your life. You were made as an image bearer of God. But sin distorts that image, like a twisted funhouse mirror. Sanctification is the process that removes that distortion so that you better reflect the image of Christ, and it requires little of you really—little more than the death of self we are talking about—because as you quit relying on yourself for life, you quit relying on yourself to take part in your own salvation. Your demise frees you from the job of savior in your own life and puts it squarely on Christ's shoulders on the cross. All human efforts to self-soothe, to comfort, to provide, to rescue ourselves from the effects of sin and misery is wasted effort that results in the sin of pride. This thought that through your own strength you can change your life, change your surroundings, change your circumstances, for a time may lead to change, but it ultimately leaves you in the same self-obsessed state you were born in.

But **to die young is to determine that all of your efforts to engineer your own life are in vain and that God is the only one who can truly set you free.** This doesn't mean that you sit back with total indifference and wait, hands folded, for the grace of God to change you. That's the cheap grace Dietrich Bonhoeffer railed against, that grace that accepts all the good from God without any action on the part of the forgiven toward repentance and devotion. This grace rejects the words in 1 Peter 1:22 that describe you as *"having purified your souls by your obedience to the truth."*

So there is a work for you to do, and it goes like this: you can't expect corn to grow in a field that you are too lazy to plant. In things of the spirit there is this rule, *"Do not be deceived: God is not mocked, for whatever one sows, that will he also reap. For the one who sows to his own flesh will from the flesh reap corruption, but the one who sows to the Spirit will from the Spirit reap eternal life. And let us not grow weary of doing good, for in due season we will reap, if we do not give up"* (Gal. 6:7–9).

Through the process of denying yourself you then sow, or plant, your spiritual nature, while simultaneously uprooting the weeds of your sinful nature as you go.

THE LIFE OF FAITH

The ideas of planting and dying are integral parts of growth, both for the garden as well as the soul. As you die, you grow in faith—as through your death God produces the fruit of righteousness. Jesus uses the example of the garden to explain this concept in regard to his own death in John 12:24, saying, *"Truly, truly, I say to you, unless a grain of wheat falls into the earth and dies, it remains alone; but if it dies, it bears much fruit."* **There is no fruit that grows from a seed that refuses to die.** And there is no spiritual growth in your life that doesn't come from your being buried in Christ. By the process of dying to yourself and your old way of life, you are brought into a new creation, one that is not only a grain but also an entire tree filled with the fruit of righteousness.

We know from experience that more wisdom and knowledge come from the hard times than the good times. We've seen it time and again. It was in the jail cell, not the winner's circle, where Michael found faith. And in the pain of the heart-wrenching rejection of a failed first engagement, Hayley was able to finally believe that no one and nothing could separate her from the love of God. We have personally seen it time and again; there isn't much growth that takes place when things are good. Why is that? It all has to do with death, because when things are bad, our weaknesses are revealed; and in those moments of weakness, those moments when what we usually rely on isn't strong enough or secure enough to see us through, our eyes finally lift their gaze off ourselves and onto the strength of God and fix on that. In those moments, as the part of us that used to serve us falls flat and lifeless and dies, it is replaced by the strength and power of the love of God. **There is a death that comes that isn't meant to destroy you but to destroy that in you which was never meant to replace the hand of God in your life.** In this comes more wisdom and growth than could ever come from the high life. So then the low life, or the death life, produces the fruit that feeds not only yourself but also those around you who see the hand of God in your life. As the tree grows out of the death of the seed, so the Spirit grows the fruit of love, joy, peace, patience, kindness, goodness, faithfulness, gentleness, and self-control out of the death of self (Gal. 5:22–23). The free flowing of these experiences, of these feelings and actions in your life, saves you from the life you had before you gave up the old ways of anger, impatience, frustration, meanness, unfaithfulness, violence, and lack of self-control and feeds those around you who are the recipients of your fruit. And, as you die young, the rocky soil of your life becomes more fertile ground for faith because the job of pleasing yourself no longer pollutes it or robs it of the nutrients of the Spirit.

THE LIFE OF LOVE

Let's face it—it's hard to love others when you love yourself more. Many believe the contrary, that you have to love yourself before you can love others. But that is the stuff of this world and not of God. While hating yourself is not a biblical concept, neither is loving yourself in order to love others. What is essential to your ability to love others is your ability to deny yourself that you might love God the most. Nowhere is this seen more beautifully than in the life of Christ, who didn't please himself (Rom. 15:2–3), but *made himself nothing, taking the form of a servant, being born in the likeness of men"* (Phil. 2:7).

In the economy of Christ, love isn't meant for self but for others. His love is a sacrificial love that didn't come to be served but to serve (Mark 10:45). And so **as we accept**

HERE LIES
HAYLEY

The part of me that had to die was the part that thought that I was in control of my own life, or rather, of my own life in the midst of natural disaster. I'm such a control freak that when things outside of my control happen, like dangerous storms, I become unglued. But when I firmly grasped the notion that nothing can happen in my life without God's permission, I was set free from the fear of being out of control, and so free to not worry, stress, or fear. And I don't think I would have grasped that concept as well had I not suffered the trials, dangers, storms, and turbulent flights.

death over life, as we die young, we die to our need to be loved so that we might love more fully. If love is about getting, then it isn't really love at all. Love is meant to be about giving. That's why love has so many commands associated with denying self. Commands like love your enemies (Matt. 5:44) mean death to your rights and even to your feelings. Commands not to insist on your own way, not to be irritable or resentful, and to endure all things (see 1 Cor. 13:4–7) mean death because doing those things is the opposite of everything your human nature believes to be good for you. Death becomes the new life of love when death takes out all the "needs" that self has when it comes to relationships. The best and most Christian love is the kind that has died to all its own concerns, plans, and needs. The love that lays down its life for its friends (John 15:13)—this is the love that is born out of the ashes of death.

THE LIFE OF PEACE

Dinner party rule number one: never talk about religion, politics, or sex. We all know the dangerous topics that send us all into battle mode. And the two most contentious topics in marriage are money and sex. When certain things come up, the gloves come off, and the ultimate fighting begins. But imagine a relationship in which winning isn't prized, the things of self aren't at stake, and self-esteem, self-worth, self-pleasure, self-respect, or proving oneself are never the goal. Would there ever be a need for a fight? Would a world built on death being the new life see friends, partners, and lovers going to war against one another? Or would the battle be over before it started?

Certainly there is no one who is perfect, not even one (Rom. 3:10). Feelings will get hurt and tempers will flare, but when the end of you is always in focus, when your self-life is prepared to be slain whenever it raises its ugly head, the battles don't last for long. **Peace attends the life of death.** It is not a cliché for nothing to say "may he rest in peace"; there is no more struggle, no more effort put on staying alive, because death has already done its work. And so when you no longer live for self, you live a life that is more peaceful than before.

THE LIFE OF HOPE

When you accept the death that no longer strives for all that God has not given, hope takes center stage. Death makes certain that life isn't the main thing anymore. Survival isn't the thing at all, but God's glory; his life is all that matters. And in that state of mind hope always wins because God always wins (1 Chron. 29:11). It is easy to become hopeless when your quality of life is of utmost importance to you. When your life is your obsession, then your hope is easily threatened because your life is easily threatened. Mountains crumble, waves crash, and people attack, but for the one who has died to the need to live for self, none of this steals hope. This person can say, *"But this I call to mind, and therefore I have hope: The steadfast love of the LORD never ceases; his mercies never come to an end; they are new every morning; great is your faithfulness. 'The LORD is my portion,' says my soul, 'therefore I will hope in him'"* (Lam. 3:21–24). **When your life and all it entails isn't your portion, but God is your portion, then it will never diminish no matter what the**

world may bring. Hope springs eternal for the one who has gone through death into life.

THE LIFE OF CHRIST

For every believer the greatest goal is to become like Christ (Rom. 8:29; 1 Cor. 11:1). His perfection, his love, his grace, his mercy, all being perfect, is then the perfect goal of his disciples. This perfect goal is the call on all believers found in Ephesians 5:1 to *"be imitators of God, as beloved children."* And any imitation of God must include this notion of death, of giving up scoring our life based on our own emotions and desires, and opting to count it all gain that is for his glory. The words penned by the apostle Paul in Philippians 3:8–11 agree with the value of dying to all that is not God when he says, *"For his sake I have suffered the loss of all things and count them as rubbish, in order that I may gain Christ and be found in him, not having a righteousness of my own that comes from the law, but that which comes through faith in Christ, the righteousness from God that depends on faith—that I may know him and the power of his resurrection, and may share his sufferings, becoming like him in his death, that by any means possible I may attain the resurrection from the dead."*

When the death to your self-life is paramount, then loss no longer concerns you, failure is irrelevant, and pain is accepted as the discipline that shapes you more into the likeness of Christ, whose suffering wasn't the result of his sin but of his love for sinners. And so it stands that your loss in death is great gain through the life of Christ who died that you may live.

THE LIFE OF PROTECTION

To die young is to become invincible to the attacks of man, because the one who has died young can no longer be separated from the love of Christ. As Romans 8:35–39 confirms:

> Who shall separate us from the love of Christ? Shall tribulation, or distress, or persecution, or famine, or nakedness, or danger, or sword? As it is written, "For your sake we are being killed all the day long; we are regarded as sheep to be slaughtered." No, in all these things we are more than conquerors through him who loved us. For I am sure that neither death nor life, nor angels nor rulers, nor things present nor things to come, nor powers, nor height nor depth, nor anything else in all creation, will be able to separate us from the love of God in Christ Jesus our Lord.

Invincible! Nothing can separate us from the love of God in Christ—nothing. And that means though people attack, though they hate, though they hurt us, the pain and suffering we endure doesn't change who we are, or whose we are, but affirms his goodness and drives us closer to him. So what they mean for evil turns out for our good. Joseph lived this idea out time and again in his lifetime. Being sold into slavery by his own brothers, being accused of a crime he never committed, being sent to jail—none of it destroyed him, none of it drove him to despair, but all of it increased his wisdom and peace. And in the end he was able to say, *"As for you, you meant evil against me, but God meant it for good"* (Gen. 50:20).

FINDING LIFE IN DEATH

So death is the new life for those who have been buried in Christ, who have given up the right to themselves and thrown themselves headlong into the arms of the Father, for you who know the truth that *"you have died, and your life is hidden with Christ in God"* (Col. 3:3), buried with him in his death and his life. And while this kind of death carries with it a lot of earthly relief, it is only the icing on the cake of salvation for the one who puts all hope on the saving power of the gospel of Christ. Now, what we have talked about in this chapter can be done without a super-natural death but through exacting devotion to following the law. There are many people who really want to obey, who believe that through obedience they will win the approval of God. They cut themselves, control them-selves, punish themselves, and strive for spiritual self-control, but the result for them is misery and sorrow because the sacrifices they make are out of the need for their salvation. But those who die young have died to their need for salvation, having turned that over to Christ through the gospel, and now can count it all joy for the sake of their love for him and not their need for salvation. When you die young, your obedience is the result of your salvation, not the cause of it.

If you only die young because you believe it will improve your life, gain you something, or get you in with God, then in the words of Oswald Chambers, it is only your "miserable commercial self-interest"[2] you are act-ing on, and the death that brings you to life is only an illusion. But to truly die young is to abandon all claim on yourself, either your improvement, salvation, or success, and to give everything to your Lord and Savior. And this can only be done by those who have been made alive by the presence of the Holy Spirit in their lives.

"Those who belong to Christ Jesus have nailed the passions and desires of their sinful nature to his cross and crucified them there." (Gal. 5:24 NLT)

CHAPTER 2

DOWN
IS THE NEW
UP

For everyone who exalts himself will be humbled, and he who humbles himself will be exalted.

LUKE 14:11

God's goal isn't to make you happy; it's to make you holy.

JAMES MACDONALD

L et's face it—it's easier to fall down than it is to get up. It's easier to descend than to climb. Gravity is against going up and insists that we all go down. But gravity isn't delicate in its insistence. It doesn't gently pull the apple from the tree; it pulls it violently to the ground leaving it bumped and bruised. It doesn't softly carry the rocks from the top of the mountain to the valley below but pushes them aggressively, gathering more and more rocks as it rushes everything in its path downward with all its force. Yes, down is easier to come by than up, but the pain that happens in the process is most of the time anything but pleasant. Drop a glass from a second-story window and see the effects of gravity in its raw and brutal strength. Gravity pulls at us all, and through strength and effort we resist it because to fall is to be scraped up and bruised. Falling, for most of us, is embarrassing. It's like when you walk down the hall and suddenly trip over nothing. Your first impulse is to look back disgustedly at the ground as if to show everyone how it reached up and grabbed you violently, leading you to stumble. Falling is no fun. It makes you look weak and vulnerable, and it's something that most of us desperately want to avoid.

But gravity will not give up. It won't let go of us easily; it's always there waiting to make fools of us, waiting to pull us back down to size, insisting that to rise again is too hard and that to try is just a waste of energy. In the words (and lyrics) of John Mayer, "Gravity is working against me, and gravity wants to bring me down,"[3] and sometimes it seems to be winning.

Down disqualifies us from the fight; it means we've lost, we've been taken down, and they've won. For the world, the idea of down is not a place most of us want to be, but in the life of faith, down isn't all that it appears to be.

Down is the new up, and it all started for the believer when Christ came to earth (Phil. 2:7–8). With his arrival, weakness became strength and death became life. His meekness confounded his followers. His kindness angered his oppressors. And his sacrifice shocked his world. He didn't live as people imagined the Messiah would. He didn't wield his omnipotence and come down from the cross, he didn't turn the rocks into bread, and he didn't beg people to follow him. He didn't disgrace sinners. He wasn't what most of the world thought he would be. Unlike a king, he owned only what he wore. Unlike royalty, he had no place to live. He didn't argue with authority but lived under it. He didn't start a rebellion but taught his followers love and sacrifice. He didn't arrive as a giant among men but as a child in a manger. God could have arranged a castle and guards for him, but he didn't even have a room. He could have had a wealthy endowment, but he was a poor carpenter. Getting the picture? Down is up and up is down. As faithful followers of Jesus,

we can't fall for the world's ideas of up when they are down.

DOWN TO SALVATION

Maybe for you, your lowest point was the doorway to your salvation. At the point that you looked at yourself and realized that you just weren't good enough, that you had failed, that you were a sinner through and through, you went down to your knees and the only place you could look was up. Michael lived a life of striving to achieve, clawing his way to the top, numbing and medicating himself on the climb, until it took a jail cell to drive him to his knees.

It's from a lowly position of self-awareness and sin that we were saved because God reaches down and touches us in our need. Jesus—the very God who left his high place and became a lowly human (Phil. 2:6–7), being unafraid to become less so that the Father could become more—met you where you were. Your down became your up. The bottom isn't such a bad place because it is only from the perspective of your own lowest point that you are able to see your sinfulness and need for a loving Savior and to be saved. It's glorious really, this fallen position where we lay ourselves out flat under the realization that we just can't do it ourselves. Coming to the end of you was the best thing you ever did, because with less of you there was more of him. And that's why down can become so much better than up.

The sudden or gradual awareness that there's more to this life than you and that you need the help of someone bigger started something in you. It started the process of bringing you down into humility. For most people humiliation is a bad thing. No one wants to be brought down or humiliated; it hurts, it's embarrassing, it's life threatening—it feels like a step toward the death we all dread. But humiliation is really just the process of someone else removing you from the throne. It's the idea of bringing you down a notch or two in power and importance, since you won't do it yourself. Humility is the foundation of all righteousness. It's our confession that we can do nothing to save ourselves and must rely fully on God for all our needs. This lowly position, which to the world might sound weak and pathetic, is really heavenly and eternal. Just as God surprises the world by making death the new life, so he confounds the world by saying that down is the new up. God says it nowhere clearer than in Luke 14:11, where he tells us that *"everyone who exalts himself will be humbled, and he who humbles himself will be exalted."* No Tower of Babel here. Up is the new down in this economy, while down is the new up. You see it? When you exalt yourself, God rewards you with humiliation. But when you humble yourself, God rewards you with exaltation. What a flip on the natural! The humble become the exalted.

WHEN DOWN IS THE NEW UP

So, what's up is down and what's down is up. But for years we believed the opposite. We heard the world's lies and fell for its ideas of upness. And we agreed that:

Success is up.

Winning is up.

Pride is up.

Control is up.

Wanting more than you have is up.

HERE LIES
MICHAEL

For years I looked for my salvation in escaping reality. My escape was gambling, and I was good at it, at least for a while. But after more than a few bad hands, and even worse decisions, I hit bottom. I needed cash and the fastest way to get it was to "borrow" it from work through cash funds or temporarily pawning electronics. Though I would return it whenever I made it back, when the business I worked for discovered my "hobby," they fired me, charged me with theft, and I hit bottom. But as they say, when you hit bottom, the only place you can look is up. From this lowest of positions I found salvation. Without my man-made mirage of a material life, the excitement and numbing effect of gambling wore off and I had nothing but him—and that was all I needed. The way down can be embarrassing, humiliating, and painful. But reaching your bottom isn't always as horrible as it looks, because when you finally stop digging, drop your shovel, and look up, you're now equipped to take the hand of the One above who is stretching out his hand to save you.

Struggling to get ahead is up.

More stuff is up.

Independence is up.

In the economy of the humanity, what looks good and feels good is up, and what hurts, looks bad, or makes you look bad is down. That's why most of us cringe when we read the words of Jesus that say, *"Do not resist the one who is evil. But if anyone slaps you on the right cheek, turn to him the other also. And if anyone would sue you and take your tunic, let him have your cloak as well"* (Matt. 5:39–40). These words are firmly rejected by most of us who, when push comes to shove, prefer standing up to backing down. So to suggest that down, in all situations, should be the new up is to suggest that life change dramatically for us all. (Read more about turning the other cheek on page 112, Turning the Other Cheek Is Weakness.)

When you die to everything that this world suggests is necessary for a "good life," when you reject everything that they say is essential for happiness, peace, or even life, you choose a road less traveled by natural man but well-traveled by the spiritual man. It is a narrow road that leads to life, and few will find it (Matt. 7:14) because few are willing to accept the paradigm shift that faith requires. This shift says that life isn't about you but about your God. That may mean taking the worst seat at the table (Luke 14:10), going the extra mile (Matt. 5:41), or forgiving someone for the same thing over and over again (Matt. 18:22). All of these the world would consider a step down in life and most definitely not a step up.

Pride is the foundation of all sin. Sin requires pride because it says "I know better than God. I must have what I must have or do what I must do." Pride puts self at

HERE LIES
MICHAEL

After just twenty-four hours of jail time following my arrest, when I was released, everything from my former life was gone except for my dog. I was completely starting over. I had lost my career, my home, and most of my friends. So for a year of my life I survived. And by "survived" I mean I found a room to rent in a softball buddy's house. I did odd jobs for his contractor business in exchange for rent until I could find a job, and for two months I lived on thirteen dollars a month for food. I would go to a grocery outlet store where they sold expiring foods or foods that didn't take off in the marketplace. I was literally a reject shopping at the reject grocery store. I would shop for almost an hour trying to find the most food for the thirteen dollars I had that day, not knowing when I'd have money again. But life on the bottom became less about embarrassment and more about redemption. When everything is stripped away, you have nothing to cling to but God and his provision and care for you. In those first years after my addiction was smashed, I learned more about life and faith than in my first three decades of life. And while those were some of the hardest times of my life, they were also the best times, because it was through them that I was reset and got to what really matters—the life of God in and through me.

HERE LIES
HAYLEY

I've always looked at life through my own eyes; all my thoughts centered only on my needs, my feelings, and my thoughts. Not out of malicious intent or a sense of superiority, but out of the continual exposure to me did I become a real high-needs woman. When going to a restaurant I was always in the habit of considering my patronage as payment enough for them to give me exactly what I wanted when I wanted it. And so upon walking into a place, my first impulse was always to ask for a booth. I wanted to make sure that wasn't by the bathroom or kitchen, and continue ordering the staff around in order to satisfy my need for comfort.

It sounds shameful when writing it down, but it was just who I was, until I started to consider what this self-preoccupation and obsession represented—my lack of love for others and my abundance of love for self. Little did I know that this kind of behavior spoke volumes of ill to those around me, revealing my sinful heart and my failure to die to self and become more like Christ.

the center of the discussion and as the idol of the heart. But in Philippians 2:3–9, pride is thrown down to the ground so that humility might be lifted up.

> Do nothing from rivalry or conceit, but in humility count others more significant than yourselves. Let each of you look not only to his own interests, but also to the interests of others. Have this mind among yourselves, which is yours in Christ Jesus, who, though he was in the form of God, did not count equality with God a thing to be grasped, but made himself nothing, taking the form of a servant, being born in the likeness of men. And being found in human form, he humbled himself by becoming obedient to the point of death, even death on a cross.

There are a couple of places in these verses where down comes up; the first and most obvious is that we are to consider others more significant than ourselves. What?! This is so unthinkable to anyone with blood pumping in their veins, (like us for instance). The guy who cuts in front of us in line sends our blood to pumping. Or the lady who thinks it's okay to stop in the middle of the street to turn left, rather than get into the actual turn lane, can make us furious. How on earth can we consider these unlikable people more significant than us? Especially when they are frustrating us?

How can we consider others more significant than ourselves and still survive? It's crazy talk. We reason that we have to be first, be fast, and be fantastic, or life is not as it should be. But that's not the way of faith. When we consider others more significant than ourselves, we

HERE LIES
MICHAEL

I am the best driver that I know. I understand the rules of the road, I respect other drivers, and I observe my surroundings, but when I'm stuck behind a slow driver, cut off by a bad driver, or in any way delayed by the antics of another person on the road, I am an angry driver. I have no patience for the lives of others, their reasons for slowing down two miles before their driveway (and not using a turn signal), or for going 15 mph in a 45. Yet when my life demands that the road take a backseat to my discussion, thoughts, or phone call, I think nothing of the man behind me. This double standard of being angry when others do the very same thing I do makes me sick. I hate the nature of my flesh which is to judge others for the very things that I do. God's Word is talking to me when it says, *"You have no excuse, O man. . . . For in passing judgment on another you condemn yourself, because you, the judge, practice the very same things"* (Rom. 2:1). I have no one to blame but myself, and nothing to claim but a severe lack of love and obsession with self that leads me to be angry when others disobey my rules of the road. To this I must die.

easily give them the right of way, we quickly give them the biggest portion and the best place, and we no longer have a need to prove ourselves, to win the argument, or to talk their ears off. And doesn't that sound good? The counterintuitive nature of taking last place is actually the remedy to all our anger, frustration, and bitterness. All of our self-protection and self-promotion comes out of our search for and/or belief in our own significance. But when we accept the notion that others matter (dare we say!) more than we do, we are freed up from the competition of life. While this initially seems dangerous to our self-life, what it ultimately does is set us free to be completely consumed with God and his will and not our own. It sets us free from our need to be anything other than a child of God. And it sets us free from the bondage of sin that attempts to raise us up on our own strength rather than the strength of the Holy Spirit that is within us. Remember that for God down is up. To let go of the need to pull yourself up, to prove yourself, or to fight for yourself is to allow God to do all that, to do the lifting; and his lifting raises you higher up than anything that you could do yourself.

With this, however, we do run the risk of making the very act of loving others *just another idol*, something that we serve even at the expense of our Father. If we choose to make others more significant than God and his Word, doing all we can to appease them, to please them, and to help them, then we are not dying to self, but serving self by placating our need to be accepted, loved, or successful in relationship to man.

In Philippians 2:4 we are told to look to our own interests as well as to those of others. With these words we

HERE LIES
HAYLEY

I've always, in every argument, considered myself more right and more significant than Michael. And because of that, I've had a really hard time getting over stuff. The slightest spat and I'm out of commission, no longer able to function as a loving and godly woman. I slam doors, I yell at our daughter, I kick the dog. Yes, I confess that I take all my pain out on others because I consider my life more significant than theirs. But when I dared to risk making Michael more important, to consider the chance that I am wrong and he is right, to give him the benefit of the doubt, and to pray "show me my error" instead of "show him his error," I was suddenly free from the sinful emotions that used to control me. And I was able to exhibit the fruit of the Spirit more abundantly than the fruit of my flesh. As counterintuitive as making others more significant is, the reward is greater than anyone can imagine.

learn the importance of standing on the foundation of faith and not allowing the interest we have in serving and obeying God to become less important than the interests of others. In this way we do what needs to be done: we work, we care for ourselves, we study, we pray, we learn, we grow. We attend to ourselves, all the while caring for the needs of others, whom we deem more significant than ourselves.

The truth is that it's easy to take this idea of insignificance so far that we pervert it and make it more about our own salvation, as we said earlier, than about loving and serving God. We've seen this kind of mistake countless times when people turn the notion of insignificance into an opportunity to punish themselves, to hate themselves, and to hurt themselves. While this may on the surface look selfless and void of vanity, if you look closely, you may see just another form of pride. Self-loathing would not exist if we had replaced our own interests with God's interests; but it does exist not solely because of our self-hatred, but because of the mostly subconscious notion that we are so significant that we ought to be doing better than we are, to be more successful than we are, to be thinner than we are, or to be in any way better than we have been. The deep-seated and camouflaged pride in us screams, "It's all about me! My pain, my suffering, my stuff. And because of that all my energy is going into fixing me, even through torture or starvation, punishment or hatred." What happens is that the punishment of self is really an elevation of self to the center of our minds.

HERE LIES
HAYLEY

There was a time in my life when I wanted to kill myself, when the voices in my head told me life was not worth living and death was the only tangible solution. But after I was talked down from the ledge, so to speak, and began to take a deeper look, not at my problems, but at God's Word, I started to see that all this drama over how miserable my life was centered on the one irrepressible idea that my miserable life wasn't worth *me* living it. I needed better, more love, more hope, more peace, more significance. It was a question of entitlement. I was entitled to a life of ease, and when I was faced with rejection by my earthly father, the loss of my loved one, and a bleak and broken future, I was so angry with my lack that I wanted revenge. This revenge was not on myself, but on everyone who had cheated me. So my self-loathing was really pride in disguise, and so it is with many of us who believe that down is the worst place that we could ever be.

A mind that puts self down where it belongs, in humility, is free to lift God up where he belongs. This kind of mind has a right assessment of self.

When we are truly honest with ourselves we can acknowledge the depth of our own sinfulness and more importantly, God's graciousness. Then self is no longer the main topic of conversation, and we are set free from needing to be anything other than a child of God. The good and the bad things in life then become, rather than success or failure, confirmation of God's Word that there is no one righteous, not even one (Rom. 3:10), and ultimately that there is no condemnation for those who are in Christ (Rom. 8:1).

In Philippians 2, the depths of Christ's humility, the Son of God putting us before himself, made him not only leave heaven and all the glory that attended him there, but also allowed him to become the servant of man. But as if that wasn't down enough, Jesus also went so far as to become *"obedient to the point of death, even death on a cross"* (Phil. 2:8). That was the lowest a man could go—pure humiliation as he hung naked on that tree.

In all he did, Christ was obedient to the Father, taking the position of servant, which was, in the eyes of the world, the lowliest position one could hold. As God became man, his journey "down" went even lower as he humbled himself to the point of death (Phil 2:8). But this death wasn't the end but the beginning. And because of his humility we have all been set free, not from obedience to God, but from obedience to sin. What remains for us, therefore, is the obedience that Christ exemplified (John 5:19). Nothing could be more backward in the modern world. Nothing more counterintuitive to success than to submit yourself to another's authority as a servant; but that's exactly the pattern we see in the life of Christ and the lives that we have been called to, once we have turned from our lives of rebellion. So humility reveals itself to be the only way up. It's the only way to elevate our God over ourselves and to serve him with complete and utter abandon. And through humility we find ourselves free from the slavery to self and to our misguided ideas of what makes for a life that is more up than down. Now that we've set humility as the new up, let's take a look at a few of the character traits of humility in the lives of believers just like you.

DOWN IS WANTING
GOD OVER HAPPINESS

On the first page of this chapter we put a quote from James MacDonald, who said that God's goal isn't to make you happy, it's to make you holy. And believe it or not, this view of faith can actually be liberating to the self-obsessed. **If we believe in the pursuit of happiness as being our right, if we elevate the idea of things going our way, of success and happiness to the point of a necessity, then we become slaves to happiness**—meaning we do whatever it takes to get it and avoid whatever threatens to take it away. In this way of living, anything other than happiness is our enemy, and because of that we scratch, claw, and fight against the pain, suffering, and sadness that is a natural part of the ebb and flow of life. But if we are willing to agree that holiness, not happiness, is the ultimate goal, then the result, ironically, will be our own happiness. It's the same down-is-up way of thinking that brings God's exaltation on our humility (Luke 14:11). In this counterintuitive move, it isn't through

DOWN IS THE NEW UP

searching for happiness but for holiness, that happiness is gained. In Psalm 37:4 this concept is laid out when it says, *"Delight yourself in the LORD, and he will give you the desires of your heart."* So **instead of delighting ourselves in our desires for happiness, we delight ourselves in him, and the result** *is* **our happiness.**

DOWN IS BEING EASILY CONTENT

The person of this world said to have discriminating or discerning taste is not easily content. They know quality and they are not happy until they get it. They rail against the waiter who serves them undercooked meat. They complain about the weather, the temperature, or the company. They turn up their noses at the wrong brand or the wrong music selections at church. They expect perfection and won't be content with anything less. For most of the Western world, being easily content is an impossibility.

Life has given us too much opportunity, too much success, and so we have made an idol of the easy life, saying things such as "I deserve it," and "I need it."

The spiritually discerning have a different standard for contentment. Rather than being hard to please, they are easily pleased. In fact, like Paul they have "learned the secret of facing plenty and hunger, abundance and need" (Phil. 4:12). They look at all things through the light of faith in the one who gives them everything, the one who strengthens them. And because of that they have everything they need in him; the rest is just runoff from their cups that overflow.

As believers die to their need to be content and happy, they find themselves miraculously content and

HERE LIES
MICHAEL

Happiness for me is eating my favorite food. I confess that at most times, food serves me better than God, because it is food that I most often go to for comfort, peace, hope, and escape from trials and suffering. When the day is done and my last nerve is shot, I have no desire to care for the temple or to eat for physical maintenance, but instead food is my salvation.

My pursuit of comfort in the form of food trumps all my logic and faith, because it is in the pursuit of food alone that I reject all that I know about what my body needs in order to perform at maximum capacity and all that is required in the form of joy and self-control in a life led by the Spirit. Instead I resort to my animal instincts for flavor and texture. This has been a struggle for me that bubbled to the surface (and my waistline) as my metabolism has slowed and my work is now tied to a keyboard. But I am determined that if I am to die young, then I must die to the areas of my life that threaten not only my physical life, but the life of God in me, in the form of devotion to something other than God himself.

HERE LIES
HAYLEY

I have good taste. I like the best brands, the best quality. I prefer organic food, natural ingredients, and good flavor. I know style and fashion, decor and design. So when I see bad taste I am disgusted. My inner most response to people with bad taste (not my taste) is disgust. I turn up my nose and shake my head. But it has occurred to me as of late that my taste is not a valid excuse for my sin of judgment and discontent.

When deciding where to go out to eat with a good friend recently I heard, "You are sure hard to please," and this truth suddenly came crashing down on me. My service to good taste subverted my service to God, and what my tongue desired became more important than fellowship and loving-kindness. This is only the tip of the iceberg of my innate desire to lift myself up and put others down (or raise them to my enlightened level!). This is my public confession of my drive to be in charge of my own destiny and to resist anything that makes me uncomfortable. Just more evidence of my need to die to my self yet again!

happy. Again, death achieves for us much more than living for ourselves ever could. So in death we are able to say, *"Who [am I] to answer back to God? Will what is molded say to its molder, 'Why have you made me like this?' Has the potter no right over the clay, to make out of the same lump one vessel for honorable use and another for dishonorable use?"* (Rom. 9:20–21). When we trust God, knowing that no matter what fate might await us, it is God who assigned it, and then we are able to be content no matter the circumstance.

DOWN IS NOT COMPLAINING

When life gets you down, the first and easiest thing to do is to complain about it. Sickness, weakness, pain, unfairness, rejection, humiliation, danger, and hunger, seem almost to demand complaint. Complaint serves to confirm the bad while glorifying the good. But complaint not only rejects the inherent badness in the situation, but proclaims the badness of the one through whom the situation came, namely God. Maybe this is why Paul urges believers to *"do everything without complaining or arguing"* (Phil. 2:14 NIV). Complaint simply elevates the one who complains, making that person the assayer of all goodness and the authority on all badness. When we put to death our need to be the authority on what's good for us and what's not, then we allow the stuff that leads to complaint to serve our righteousness rather than destroy it. Just remember that **complaint is our crying out for heaven on earth combined with the assumption that we deserve it.** The suffering that leads to complaint is far better used to bring us down than as a commentary on why we should be up.

DOWN IS THE NEW UP

DOWN IS NOT NEEDING TO BE HEARD

One of the most uncomfortable things in the world is speaking and not being heard. When others ignore you or refuse to listen, your ability to prove yourself, to be understood, to gain favor, to show off, to succeed, and to win are all lost. When they don't hear you, it's as if you aren't there, as if you don't matter. And so being heard is of utmost importance in every relationship on earth. But speaking can easily get out of control when its main goal is anything to do with self. Proverbs warns us about talking too much with these words: "*When words are many, transgression is not lacking, but whoever restrains his lips is prudent*" (10:19).

DOWN IS NOT NEEDING TO WIN

When you die young, you die to your need to be first. In the parable of the laborers, Jesus tells the story of day workers who were jealous after receiving the same pay as the workers who had worked less than half the time they had. The master of the house explains that his generosity is his concern and not theirs, and then Jesus makes this impossible statement that "*the last will be first, and the first last*" (Matt. 20:16). And again God turns the world's economy of right and just on its ear. Winning isn't everything anymore; in fact, it could be called losing in this line of thinking. Winning and the thrill of victory put all the emphasis on being first, on being the best, and outdoing everyone else. But God wants us to be careful of boasting, of being filled with pride, and of bragging on our victory and instead wants us to boast about our weaknesses (2 Cor. 12:9) and to look for the good of our

HERE LIES
MICHAEL

In any argument with Hayley, I really want to be heard. Nothing is more uncomfortable than her interrupting me or not listening to what I am saying. I used to throw my hands up in the air and walk out if she interupted or drifted off, until I realized that her way of listening was hyperactive listening, aka talking along with me. Needing to be heard is a strong desire for me. If people won't listen, then I'm prone to be angry because I feel a deep need to convince them of my knowledge and their error. I have little faith in God to do that for me, to work things out, to speak to the heart of anyone but me, and so I talk, lecture, and pontificate, meticulously communicating so that everything will be worked out and I am perfectly understood. When being heard, speaking everything you feel or believe is no longer paramount, but silence and listening become the mainstays of your life. Congratulations, you've embraced down as the new up. That's when you can "let another praise you, and not your own mouth; a stranger, and not your own lips" (Prov. 27:2). When you can refuse the need to dump your emotions onto man for relief, but instead go to God and listen quietly at his feet, then down is a great place to find yourself. In these moments when you deny yourself such a basic human desire, you die to your urges and you live for every word that comes out of the mouth of God. As Jesus said in the desert when being tempted by Satan, "Man shall not live by bread alone, but by every word that comes from the mouth of God" (Matt. 4:4). You cannot hear the words that come from the mouth of God while you are talking. For the most part, our words lift us up, while his words lift him up. So when you turn down your word count, you turn up his and down becomes the new up.

neighbors over ourselves (1 Cor. 10:24). And violà, down is the new up.

It's human nature to look out for ourselves, to find our own advantages, and to position ourselves for success. While success in the areas of faith, service, and obedience is of great gain, the pursuit of earthly success is counterintuitive to a life bent on serving God and his children. Nowhere is this idea of serving God and others over self more evident than in the life of the apostle Paul, who was so set on the salvation and maturing of others in Christ that he even wished that he were *"accursed and cut off from Christ"* for the sake of his brothers, the Israelites (Rom. 9:3–4). This notion that we are nothing and others are something is what allows us to love the unlovely—something that is impossible if we think too highly of ourselves. But Paul tells us, *"Let no one seek his own good, but the good of his neighbor"* (1 Cor. 10:24). In fact, he goes on to say that he himself attempts to please everyone in everything he does as he says, *"Not seeking my own advantage, but that of many, that they may be saved"* (1 Cor. 10:33).

This has to be one of the most unsafe feelings emanating from the commands of Scripture—looking out for others instead of ourselves. We are parents of a six-year-old, so asking us to look out for the good of others hits us really hard when we see our daughter getting the worst. Whenever she is in a line and gets pushed to the end and cries, everything in us wants to push her right back to the front. When she is given the ugliest party favor, the smallest piece of cake, or the worst seat, our natures want to stand up and demand better. But this idea that we deserve better is at the heart of all that is selfish and

therefore sinful. And truth be told, it takes a strong redirecting of our minds to put us back to thinking more like sinners saved by grace than royalty destined for only the best of things.

DOWN IS NOT FEARING FAILURE

When we lose or fail, we can feel as though we've let ourselves down. But that way of thinking continues to make life about us. In order to make good sense of our falling down, we have to assign the same value to our failure that God assigns in the form of the discipline that teaches and purifies us when we allow our mistakes to be redeemed. As it says in Hebrews 12:11, *"For the moment all discipline seems painful rather than pleasant, but later it yields the peaceful fruit of righteousness to those who have been trained by it."* The down of the discipline of failure is meant for your good, and so why would you fear it? But know that its yield is the peaceful fruit of righteousness, and be trained by your failure rather than destroyed by it. When we let down do its work, up will be the result.

DOWN IS NOT REQUIRING PERFECTION

Written in red letters in Matthew 5:48 are the words, *"You therefore must be perfect, as your heavenly Father is perfect."* While perfection, or Christlikeness, is something we all should strive for, being a perfectionist is something different and much more human. Perfectionists need perfection in order to feel acceptable, successful, or good. They use perfection as a replacement for salvation, turning to it for all that God himself has done. But this command by Jesus is talking about how we are to love others, not ourselves. It is not saying

HERE LIES
HAYLEY

For most of my life I've been a complainer—big surprise. But it's because I felt my complaint was just being honest and intimate with others, sharing my innermost thoughts. "Thanks for the backrub," I would say to Michael, "but couldn't it be longer?" "Movie? You call that a movie? What a waste of your money, honey." When I felt something, I spoke it. Made sense to me. But what I didn't know was that complaint not only revealed my sinful and discontent heart, but that it also spoke accusation not only toward God but toward whoever was trying to take care of me.

SORE WINNERS

One of the dangers of winning is the need to rejoice over our betterness—the victory dance, the self-appreciation, "We're number one!" "Boo-hoo for you!" "Na-na-na-na, hey-hey-hey, goodbye!" All convey our self-obsession and dismissal of others. We crave victory in order to prove our worth and your worthlessness. We make others feel smaller so we feel bigger. But is wanting to win, or at least savoring it so, a godly response to competition? Or does it betray our pride and obsession?

that only through perfection can you be acceptable or righteous. The love that God shares with us is perfect, unselfish, faithful, hopeful, and generous, so our love should be the same.

Perfectionists look to the perfect completion of an activity or task in their lives to lift themselves up. But those who have died to their own abilities to perfect their lives bring their lives down so that the Holy Spirit in them has the sole responsibility to lift them up and perfect them. For perfectionists, the life verse that speaks to freedom is Galatians 1:10, which asks, *"Am I now seeking the approval of man, or of God? Or am I trying to please man?"* Then after asking this question, the answer to the dilemma of perfection is given, *"If I were still trying to please man, I would not be a servant of Christ."* And pleasing man includes pleasing ourselves by pleasing others that we might feel accepted, admired, or accomplished. Perfectionists are obsessed not with pleasing God, but man, both themselves and others. This idolatry worships achievement as our savior. But this is upside-down thinking that results in your up becoming your down. To be set free from the sin of perfectionism, learn to reject the demands of self that require perfect execution of a thing in order to be deemed perfect.

DOWN IS THE ONLY WAY UP

Pride never saves anyone but yourself, and it really doesn't even do that. Some might say national pride and patriotism save, as soldiers proudly go to war for their country. But is it really pride that says "I'll go," or humility that says, "More lives are worth more than mine, so I will go"? **Humility saves others**. It was the humility of

Christ, being willing to become a man and to die on a cross, that led to our salvation. Without his humbling himself and becoming a man, our salvation would be left in our own hands.

But pride kills. Pride makes man the center of his own universe and the idol of his heart. God promises a swift trip down from this self-raised position when he says *"Pride goes before destruction, and a haughty spirit before a fall"* (Prov. 16:18). The very act of lifting ourselves up ultimately brings us down, while the act of bringing ourselves down does the opposite—it lifts us up. *"The reward for humility and fear of the LORD is riches and honor and life"* (Prov. 22:4).

Down is the new up in the life of faith. What used to be good for the old man is offensive to the new man. The whole world is turned upside down when you die young and determine to live for the One who died for you.

HERE LIES
MICHAEL

When you experience a public failure as big as mine, if you come out of it with a new and stronger faith, you learn never to fear failure again. Failure used to be not an option for me, but now I see the value in failure. I can credit my failure with my salvation. And while I don't go out looking for failure, I don't fear it either. When I used to fear failure, I had to medicate (gamble) in order to try to avoid it. But when I lost my fear of failing, I no longer needed medication, but a sober reliance on the God who is always with me, even through the failures in which many had abandoned me.

HERE LIES
MICHAEL

Most of my life I have been a people pleaser. I have done all I can to make the people in my life happy so that they will like me. I always knew about my tendency to please, but it wasn't till recently that I figured out that my pleasing was actually causing me and my loved ones more pain than anything else. Because in my effort to please was couched resentment for having to please. Subconsciously I blamed those I worked so hard to please for my desire to please them. Twisted, I know. But once I let go of this incessant need to please, my relationships got healthier, and the stress, frustration, and strains of life lessened for me. Now I live to please God, and that takes care of all the rest.

CHAPTER 3

LESS
IS THE NEW
MORE

There is within the human heart a tough fibrous root of fallen life whose nature is to possess, always to possess. It covets "things" with a deep and fierce passion.

A. W. TOZER

It's not those of us who have nothing but those of us who wish for more who are poor.

HAYLEY & MICHAEL DIMARCO

Y ou're gonna have to learn to live on less."
    "Your portion is smaller, your house is smaller,
your desk is smaller."

"You get less than he does."

"More for me, less for you."

Part of the death that leads to righteousness (Rom.
6:16) as you die young is learning to die to your desire for
stuff—the definition of stuff being anything other than
God. And **while stuff isn't inherently evil, the position
we give it in our hearts can be**.

Face it—less isn't something most of us are excited
about getting, unless it's less of something bad. When it
comes to the good stuff, more is always better. More
money is always better than less money. More comfort
is better than less comfort. More fun is preferable to less
fun. And more possessions are better than fewer possessions. More makes sense. In fact, the world judges people by how much more they have. We idolize and want to
be like the rich and famous. The Fortune 500, the Forbes
400—we envy people with more square footage and
more closet space. As believers we often want more so
that we can give more, help more, and do more. Less is
never our plea or our supplication. "Dear God, please

HERE LIES
HAYLEY

I have always believed in the concept of more; in fact less to me is a crime. Like when I used to make a pie, I could not eat less than half of it at one sitting. Less than that is just a tease, agony. I want more, always more. In fact, it takes a good deal of self-control for me not to eat the entire pie in one day. I have a hard time with less.

HERE LIES
MICHAEL

When it comes to stuff, I'm not immune to its charms. I love stuff. Electronic stuff, sweet stuff, fast stuff. And the more stuff the better, as far as I'm concerned. I love creating stuff and consuming others' creations. But the more I stuff my life with the creations of creation, the less I'm mindful of the Creator.

give me less good stuff," probably has never been your prayer.

The truth is when we like something, we want more of it. If we like one Precious Moments figurine, we want more Precious Moments figurines. If we like owning one movie, we want to own more movies. When something is good, the human mind wants more. So it all comes down to the good we desire. We see something; it's good, and so we decide increase is essential. But this can become a dangerous concept when abundance is accepted as the norm. For the eater, more can lead to physical trouble. For the consumer, more can lead to financial strain. For the lover, more can lead to heart and health problems. For everything that we want more of, there is an accompanying danger in the more.

The danger really isn't even with the stuff but with the position that our hearts give the stuff. There is nothing inherently wrong or sinful with houses, cars, relationships, clothes, or food, but when we look to those things to provide any or all of what God means to provide, then we have a spiritual problem. See, **in the universe there is only God and stuff**—stuff that he created and stuff his creation created. And we can look to one or the other to meet our needs, but we can't look to both. So when we look to stuff for comfort, fulfillment, validation, protection, and joy, we look away from God for the very things he's promised to bring to our lives. And suddenly the stuff around us becomes our little gods, protecting and providing for our every need. Maybe that's why God's Word has such strong commands about stuff. In 1 John 2:15–17 we read these harsh-sounding words to a world obsessed with the things of this world:

Do not love the world or the things in the world. If anyone loves the world, the love of the Father is not in him. For all that is in the world—the desires of the flesh and the desires of the eyes and pride in possessions—is not from the Father but is from the world. And the world is passing away along with its desires, but whoever does the will of God abides forever.

"The world is passing away," dying, and that means we can either die with it or to it. When you refuse to die to the world you automatically choose to die with it. And so it pulls you down into the death of hope, peace, trust, and even faith as you attempt to find all of those in the stuff of this world that will soon perish. But to die to the world and the need for stuff is to die young and to believe that less is more. It's the belief that less of this world is more of God—and even that less on this earth means more of the things of heaven.

While the world is obsessed with getting more, God cares about giving more. Stuff, the things of this world that we want and need, isn't meant to be stored up and collected for our happiness and protection, but to be given away, and invested—not in our future here on earth but our future in heaven. Jesus said, "*Sell your possessions, and give to the needy. Provide yourselves with moneybags that do not grow old, with a treasure in the heavens that does not fail, where no thief approaches and no moth destroys. For where your treasure is, there will your heart be also*" (Luke 12:33–34).

The trouble with more is that it is a treasure problem. The more you have of something, or the more you want something that you don't have, the more you treasure it. According to Jesus what you treasure points to what or whom you love. We tend to put our affections on our treasures. Look up the word "treasure" in a thesaurus and see words like, "cherish," "adore," "dote," and "worship." Thinking about treasure this way helps you see the problem, or at least it should. Less is the new more because the less we treasure, cherish, and worship here on earth, the more our hearts yearn for the things of heaven, that is, God and his will.

The truth is that with less of us there is more room for God and his will. When there is more of us the space left for God is greatly diminished. In the end self wins. But less leads to more in the life of faith. John the Baptist, the announcer of the Savior, understood this perfectly when he said of Christ, *"He must become greater and greater, and I must become less and less"* (John 3:30 NLT). And so less of you means more of him. Less of your strength means more of his (2 Cor. 12:9–10). And less of your will leads to more of his.

Less becomes more when less is a rejection of all that is unholy, unbiblical, and disobedient. Less cake is more self-control. Less doubt is more faith. Less fear is more trust. The less we allow ourselves to follow our desire and passion for the more of this world, for the more that sin offers, the more we have of God himself (1 John 2:15–17). So taking less and allowing less stuff to become important is to find more than we ever imagined. Less is the new more because of what less of this earth allows for. It allows for the more of him who inhabits heaven.

WHY LESS?

As we've said, the danger of stuff isn't inherent in the stuff. There are plenty of pursuits in this world that are good when consumed in moderation. Plenty of healthy activities such as church, hobbies, relationships, even Bible study, are good stuff in the life of faith. But the trouble with the world's idea of more being better is that the more we need these things in our lives, the more we rely on them to be what God himself is meant to be, and thus, the more we end up worshiping the creation rather than the Creator.

God is a jealous God. He won't stand for rivals. One translation of Exodus 20:5 reads, *"Do not make for your-selves images of anything in heaven or on earth or in the water under the earth. Do not bow down to any idol or worship it, because I am the Lord your God and I tolerate no rivals"* (GNT). A rival to God, then, would be anything or anyone who competes for his place in your life to do what he himself promises to do for us. So if there is anything in our lives that does the job of God or that we go to for the things of God, then we have become idolaters. This isn't an ancient concept reserved for little golden idols or pendants carved of wood and worshiped as protector or provider but is something that all of us fall prey to regularly. All of us who indulge in the idea that less just isn't enough, who crave more than we need of something, or who agree with the world's idea of self-satisfaction at all costs have created for ourselves idols.

If you aren't sure about this idea yet or don't understand what God considers a rival, then take a look at this list of what God promises to do for you, and see if there is anything else in your life that has taken his place.

Both God and idols promise to:

Make you feel better (2 Cor. 7:6–7)

Give you approval (2 Cor.10:18)

Meet all your needs (Phil. 4:19)

Forgive your sins (Eph. 1:7)

Give you hope (Ps. 62:5)

Save you (Rom. 6:22; 10:9)

Rescue you (Ps. 22:5)

Protect you (Ps. 18:2)

Accept you (Rom. 5:10)

Heal you (Ps. 103:3)

Complete you (Ps. 20:4)

Not condemn you (John 3:18)

Relieve your distress (2 Thess. 3:16)

Tell you what to do to be happy (Ps. 37:4)

Occupy all your thoughts (Mark 12:30)

Demand your undying allegiance
(Matt. 6:24; Jer. 7:23)

When less is more, stuff takes its rightful place. It becomes less about meeting our wants and more about being thankful for what God has provided. **As long as we continue to hoard the things that God has given us, we keep those things from changing the lives of those around us.** To give stuff its rightful place is to determine that the purpose of all the stuff in this world is to glorify God. Imagine if all your stuff served no other purpose than God's glory; how much differently would you use your stuff? How much of your stuff would you consider more important to be given than to be kept? What if the stuff you have was given to you, not as a final destination, but as a pit stop on the way to someone else in need?

HERE LIES
HAYLEY

I have discovered an idol in my life—something I go to for comfort and peace, something I give credit to for bringing me out of my funk. It is shopping therapy. Buying things is a drug. It heals the soul; at least it feels like it. And I confess to you that I am an addict. I shop to feel good. I shop to quench my thirst for more. I shop to avoid suffering and fatigue and to be content in my life. The more I buy, the better I feel, at least for the moment, but soon all that stuff starts to make me feel bloated and out of control. I ask myself why I look to stuff to meet my needs when God is all-sufficient. I guess I have yet to fully believe it, as long as I go elsewhere for the "more" of life that I desire.

Thinking that the stuff around you is meant to complete you or to fully satisfy you is wrong thinking. Jesus turns this human idea upside down when he tells us, *"Whoever would save his life will lose it, but whoever loses his life for my sake will find it"* (Matt. 16:25). This saving of your life through the stuff you put into it is then turning away from God and his saving grace and toward the saving grace of stuff. And this is the essence of idolatry.

THE NEW MORE

"You are not restricted by us, but you are restricted in your own affections" (2 Cor. 6:12). **The less there is that competes for our attention and favor in life, the more attention and favor we can give to God.** The life of less, one bent on simplicity, and not needing or wanting anything other than what God has deemed good for you turns out to be all you could ever need or want. With this idea of dying to all that self might require that is inconsistent with the life of Christ in you comes all kinds of spiritual and emotional growth. So let's take a look at some of the more that less can become when it's less of you and more of him.

MORE SURRENDER

When you die young, you surrender your will to the will of God. You abandon yourself to something, or rather Someone, who is more important and significant than yourself. Less is more in this scenario because less concern for self-protection, self-esteem, and self-worth yields more than those efforts on their own ever could. See, surrender means not only that you've come to terms with the idea that life isn't about you but also that you see the benefit in that notion. As long as you're working to get more peace, more happiness, more hope, or more love, you are living in your own strength, insisting that your will is not only the most important will for you but also the essential will for your life. And while this way of thinking can work for a while, giving you some good results, ultimately living to serve yourself is futile. It separates you from the One whose will for your life is not only all-perfect but also completely sufficient to provide for that will.

When less becomes more, less of what you want matters, and more of what he wants becomes the goal. In this surrendered state, then, success is a sure thing, because the one you've surrendered to has both the will and the power to achieve it. **With more surrender there is less to worry about.** Doubt that? Then *"look at the birds of the air: they neither sow nor reap nor gather into barns, and yet your heavenly Father feeds them"* (Matt. 6:26). There is no battle in them for their will over the Father's. They surrender their lives to doing what they were made to do. Surrender might sound like defeat, but it is really victory when the one you surrender to is the only One who has the power to save you.

MORE SELF-CONTROL

When less of this world is what you want, more self-control is what you get. Self-control has great value not only for your waistline but also for your soul. The lack of self-control among believers has become an acceptable sin. We accept it as a weakness, as a struggle that we all have and so we have to live with it. But God wants us to be free from the control of our passions and lusts for the

HERE LIES
HAYLEY

My surrender came when we moved from our 3,000–square-foot house into a 200–square-foot motor home. We were going to live life on less, on the road as a family for three months, and I could take with us only what we needed. This was a very grueling job for me. Giving up all the comforts of home scared me. So I had to surrender my needs and trust that less would be more for us. In the end it turned out that was true. Our family thrived with less. Cleaning dishes only took me five minutes because we had only one dish and one fork for each of us. Our days were spent sitting next to one another because there was no place else to go. Giving up our stuff and surrendering our need for comfort, luxury, and space brought us closer together than we ever could have imagined. Now we see stuff for what it is, useful to bring God glory, but unnecessary to bring us joy.

things of this world. He wants us to develop self-control (2 Pet. 1:5–6), to practice it (1 Pet. 1:7), and to let it grow in our lives as a fruit of the Spirit (Gal. 5:22–23).

Ironically, self-control comes from death—death to everything that sets itself up as our master, including our wants and needs. When you die young, you are able to put yourself under the control of the Holy Spirit, so less is more because less of you is more of him. Self-control is easy for the person who has decided that pleasing self isn't at the top of the list, but controlling self is all-important. When that's your goal, then less becomes a valuable tool in that practice. To deny yourself something, anything, even if it isn't something bad for you (think fasting or the practice of Lent) is to teach yourself that you will not be controlled by your passions.

Less is more because the **continual practice of less keeps your wants from becoming your needs.** The only stuff you need as a human being is water, food, and shelter. Without those you will die. But above that everything else is a want. When you lack self-control and when more is always better, what you want quickly becomes essential to your life, or at least you convince yourself so. And in that moment what you want/need becomes your master demanding to be served.

Less is more because an understanding of the value of less stuff in your life leads to more of what you really need, God's presence and will. **When less is offensive, when less makes you uncomfortable, God becomes less important than your need for more.** But less blesses those who allow it to make God everything that is needed. Self-control grows out of this understanding that less is more and that determining to deny yourself, or to die to self, is the quickest way to place God back on the throne of your life.

MORE TIME FOR
WHAT REALLY MATTERS

An emphasis on less leads to more time for what really matters. With less to manage, less to protect, and less to worry about, more important things can be attended to. When stuff is the main focus of a mind, that mind is divided, and what really matters is neglected. One of the most often misquoted verses of Scripture says this: *"The love of money is a root of all kinds of evils. It is through this craving that some have wandered away from the faith and pierced themselves with many pangs"* (1 Tim. 6:10). Most people misquote this and simply say that money is the root of all evil. But they miss a very important ingredient in this evil; it isn't the money itself, which is neither good nor evil, but it is our relationship with money that counts. The "love" of money itself is the problem. When we love something we want more of it, we dream about it and talk about it all the time. We become obsessed over the things or people that we love, and we want more, more, more. But **becoming content with less is the only way that we ever get enough.** Money will always be lacking and so will love as long as we give in to our cravings. But less is actually more when through death we kill the need for stuff to complete us, to rescue us, or to comfort us.

When you can become content with less you will find more time for what really matters. More time for prayer, more time for serving, more time for loving, more time for hope, and more time for study. Understanding the value of less stuff sets you free to enjoy the things in life that really matter—the people, the relationships, the rest that comes from a heart set fully on God and his will and not on you and yours.

MORE REST

Accumulation requires work. The more you have, the more work—the more you want, the more work. Work, work, work. But less means more rest because there is less stuff to take care of. The stuff we are talking about isn't just material possessions, which do require a lot of energy just to gain and maintain, but also the stuff of relationships, success, hobbies, anything that requires your mind, space, and/or time. Researchers tell us that almost **60 percent of Christians around the world feel like busyness gets in the way of their relationship with God,** keeping them from having enough time for him.[5] This just proves that the world's idea that more is always better is a broken idea. In the life of faith, more is less and less is more. It's another flip, where what makes sense is crazy, but what is crazy is true. **Less is more in the life of faith because with less to do, to think, and to want there is more time for the things that really matter.**

"I'll rest when I'm dead" takes on a whole new and exciting meaning when you consider the death of the self-life. You truly can rest when you are dead to all the yearnings, pleadings, and demands of self. Less life equals more life when you exchange your life for his, and more of the life of Christ in you means more rest for your soul.

Jesus confirms this in Matthew 11:28, when he says, *"Come to me, all who labor and are heavy laden, and I will give you rest."* Under what and with what are we so heavy laden? Stuff, it's stuff, all that stuff that isn't God that we labor so hard with—the stuff we worry about and work for, that holds us down and makes us tired. But the burden of Jesus is easy. *"For my yoke is easy, and my burden is light,"* he goes on to say in verse 30. That doesn't mean that obedience and faith are easy, but living under the yoke with Jesus next to you means that it isn't through your strength or power that you do all that you do, but through his. And in this there is rest because it becomes less about you and more about him.

MORE GIVING

One of the strongest motivations of human nature is self-protection. It means our survival, and because of that we are continually working on how to get what we need in order to survive. If you are honest with yourself, on any given day most of your thoughts go into getting what you need to eat, to sleep, to work, to buy, to clean, to love. **The natural state of man is to concentrate on getting what we need.** Getting is good; in fact when we get a nice gift, or when unexpected money comes our way we are thankful for the "blessing" that God has provided; and while that's true, everything comes from God and is a blessing for those who receive it. This is also another case where what's less is more and what's more is less. And here's how it goes: we've all heard it before, the words written in red in Acts 20:35, *"It is more blessed to give than to receive."* But try to convince a six-year-old of this fact and find out how counterintuitive it really is. It makes no sense to the natural mind; how can giving ever be better than getting? Giving means less for you and more for them, and that doesn't fit with human self-interest and self-protection. More is always better, or so it seems.

But **it is that deep desire within us to get more that giving is meant to kill.** The Bible has a word for the desire for more—covetousness, wanting what you don't have. For most of us that's just another one of those acceptable sins. **We know the word "covet" is bad, but when we see something we really want, complain because we don't have it, or do all we can to get it, we give it a completely different definition. "Need," "deserve," "meant for,"** are the terms we use to define the desires of our hearts.

Jesus warns us about wanting what we don't have in Luke 12:15 when he gives this warning: *"Take care, and be on your guard against all covetousness, for one's life does not consist in the abundance of his possessions."* **The "more" of life doesn't come from more stuff but from more God.** And giving others our stuff, having less for ourselves, gives us more than we could ever imagine, not only in righteousness and obedience, but also in giving not only to man but also to God. As Jesus said, *"Truly, I say to you, as you did it to one of the least of these my brothers, you did it to me"* (Matt. 25:40). Death to self through giving, not getting, has the reward of serving and loving Christ himself. Being bent on doing what you've been gifted to do for the children of God here on earth serves our Father in heaven.

MORE LOVE

The more stuff that we have around us or within us in the form of desire or obsession, the less capable we are of loving people. This is because to love another human being requires that we place our focus on that human being and not on our stuff. Less is more love because with less of the stuff that satisfies and occupies self the more room there is for love Him. As Scripture tells us, *"God is love"* (1 John 4:8), and in order for us to love we must have room in our hearts for God himself. Stuff can crowd out the space in our hearts and leave only a sliver for the things of love. But when we die to our need for more stuff and instead live off of less, we find a stronger capacity to love, more time to love, and more love to give. Less is more because loving the concept of "less" stuff helps us to stop living for ourselves and to love others the way Christ loves us, selflessly. Less is more in the life of love because it allows for less competition for our affection and more time for the things of love.

MORE PEACE

Consider your lack of peace. What does it come from? From the idea that you might not get something you want? Or that you might lose something that you love? Much of the unrest in our lives comes from our thoughts on the importance of all that isn't God himself. But the peace that God offers comes from putting him on the throne, instead of yourself and your wants. In this putting down of your will and lifting up of his, everything he allows is deemed the best; and when the best comes in the form of loss, danger, or failure, peace is still attainable because it relies solely on the desires of God and not of self. When that is your state of mind then you can, as Paul put it, *"not be anxious about anything, but in everything by prayer and supplication with thanksgiving let your requests be made known to God. And the peace of*

God, which surpasses all understanding, will guard your
hearts and your minds in Christ Jesus" (Phil. 4:6–7).

Both peace and your ability to give up being anxious
in order to solve a problem or improve a situation sur-
pass all understanding because from a human perspective they are illogical. It makes sense to worry and to
stress; it feels like taking action where no other action
can be taken. But in the realm of faith, action is best taken
when it is trust in the God who moves mountains rather
than in fear that the mountain he won't move will be the
end of you. Less of your effort, and less thinking that it's
through your strength that good comes to pass, leads to
more peace, because you can't manufacture peace
through all your worry and fear. It's only through faith in
the Prince of Peace. When you have that, then his peace
will be yours no matter the situation.

MORE BLESSING

A. W. Tozer once said that "the blessed ones who possess the Kingdom are they who have repudiated every
external thing and have rooted from their hearts all sense
of possessing,"[6] In other words, they have determined
that less is truly more. Tozer can say this with confidence
because of Jesus's words in the Beatitudes listed in Luke
6:20–23 where we read:

> *Blessed are you who are poor, for yours is the*
> *kingdom of God. Blessed are you who are hungry*
> *now, for you shall be satisfied. Blessed are you*
> *who weep now, for you shall laugh. Blessed*
> *are you when people hate you and when they*
> *exclude you and revile you and spurn your name*
> *as evil, on account of the Son of Man! Rejoice*

in that day, and leap for joy, for behold, your
reward is great in heaven; for so their fathers did
to the prophets.

These words turn the ideas of man upside down. What kind of happiness or blessing could come from less money, less food, less laughter, and less adoration? Jesus seems to be saying that true happiness isn't rooted in the abundance of stuff but in the lack of stuff. He's offering more happiness—another way of saying "blessing"—to all who would have less.

The blessings of God come to those who find
nothing more valuable than doing his will. Unstuff,
making room in your life for what really matters.

In every blessing there is less, less of you; but there is also more, more happiness and more hope than can be found in any of the stuff you used to go to for those things. Less, in another plot twist, turns to more when you no longer respond to the part of you that seeks to please self, when instead you put that part to death and bury yourself in Christ.

MORE FAITH

Jesus taught that *"it is easier for a camel to go through the eye of a needle than for a rich person to enter the kingdom of God"* (Mark 10:25). Many think this is because riches are a symbol of greed and sin, and while this is often the case, **it might well be that the rich person has such a hard time entering heaven because seemingly there is no need for it**. We have a relative who has millions of dollars. He is a very successful man in the world's eyes, but ask him about Jesus and he says, "What do I need him for? I have enough money to buy whatever I want." When we have all that we need or want in this life, there is little room left for faith. Maybe that's why we see such incredible displays of faith in parts of the world where the church is persecuted. These people who have very little of what they need, and almost nothing of what they want, are blessed with the kind of faith that gives them the strength to endure what most of us never could and the ability to do what only the early church did.

Not that we are proposing that we all look to move to areas of persecution and famine, but there is something to be said about a healthy understanding of less being more. When more is always at your fingertips, when more is the answer to everything that ails you, then you no longer need Jesus. And when you no longer need Jesus, it is because you have turned to other gods.

The very state of having less requires faith—faith that you will survive, faith that God is sufficient, and faith that perseverance is part of godliness. **When you look at your lack as something to be bemoaned, or when you feel envy over what you don't have that others do, you are accusing God of deceit and of failing to come through on his promises.** But a healthy understanding of the principle of less being more will set you free from the bonds of resentment, fear, and envy.

LESS IS MORE

In a world where we measure success by how much money we have and fulfillment by how much happiness we have, it's easy to look for more stuff in order to be successful and fulfilled. But more stuff isn't the answer to the deeper problem of our souls. Less is more for the souls that consider their gain nothing compared to the riches in Christ. When less is more you can honestly say these words written from a man under arrest found in Philippians 3:8–9:

> *Indeed, I count everything as loss because of the surpassing worth of knowing Christ Jesus my Lord. For his sake I have suffered the loss of all things and count them as rubbish, in order that I may gain Christ and be found in him, not having a righteousness of my own that comes from the law, but that which comes through faith in Christ, the righteousness from God that depends on faith.*

In the life of Paul we can vividly see the life of less being more than we could ever imagine because he suffered the loss of all things; but that didn't make him mourn. Instead, it led him to call all that stuff "rubbish" in comparison with knowing Christ and being found in him. So, too, for you less can become more than you ever imagined when you die young and refuse to live a minute longer for yourself.

Our woes began when God was forced out of His central shrine and 'things' were allowed to enter. Within the human heart `things' have taken over. Men have now, by nature, no peace within their hearts, for God is crowned there no longer, but there in the moral dusk, stubborn and aggressive usurpers fight among themselves for first place on the throne.

A. W. TOZER[4]

CHAPTER 4

WEAK
IS THE NEW
STRONG

*I think God was looking for a little man, little enough so that
He could show Himself strong through him. A man can
receive nothing, except it be given him from heaven.*
HUDSON TAYLOR, EXPLAINING HIS SUCCESS

*For the sake of Christ, then, I am content with weaknesses,
insults, hardships, persecutions, and calamities.
For when I am weak, then I am strong.*
2 CORINTHIANS 12:10

Death generally follows a period of weakness. It may be long or short, by cancer or by car crash. But in all instances, our death proceeds from our weakness. Our bodies are not immortal but prone to injury and death. Charles Darwin is credited with teaching generations to believe that death ultimately comes quickly to the weak and more slowly to the strong. The survival of the fittest in the animal kingdom proves this and is evidence, then, of the value of strength. Strength leads to more life. And because of this the world has coveted strength since the beginning of time.

Our first parents ate from the tree of the knowledge of good and evil, perhaps believing that this knowledge would give them strength. As it is said, "knowledge is power." And power is reserved for the strong under the law of nature. Even Satan himself, when determining to take the place of God, wanted ultimate power unequalled by any. It is God's nature, and his alone, to be all-powerful, yet people since the dawn of time have sought to become like God, to reach up to heaven and to seize his very essence. In Genesis 11:1–9 we read the story of Babel, the city whose name means the "gate of god." The city is known for its tower, erected as an attempt to build a way to heaven, to seize God's power, and to become all-sufficient.

Since the dawn of time, strength has been a yardstick of success. Strength is bragged about by the strong and dreamt of by the weak. We make heroes of strong men who consistently defeat weaker men and of strong nations that rise above the weak peoples of the world. Weak is another one of those ugly words that people don't want to hear about themselves. Who wants to be considered weak? The weak man is pitied. The weak woman, who can stand? But strength? Strength is coveted.

Strength is not available to everyone, however, and it isn't without end. When you walk or run, you go from strength to weakness. Energy and strength decrease over time and exertion. That's the natural state of things. Age does the same thing; the young man is stronger than the old man, able to rebound from injury, to endure more strain on his body. As we age we are less and less able to withstand, as our strength diminishes with time. That's why it is such good news that weak is the new strong, because as we are weak and insist that God is our strength we, like the *"blessed"* of Psalm 84, *"go from strength to strength,"* (Ps. 84:7) rather than from strength to weakness. We *"mount up with wings like eagles,"* we run and don't grow weary; we walk and don't grow faint (Isa. 40:31). The irony in all of this is that God gives strength to the weak, to the faint, not to the strong.

The life of Jesus exemplifies this, the all-powerful One reaching down into the world to exchange first strength for weakness, through becoming a man and suffering torture and death on the cross, then to exchange our weakness for his strength, through the resurrection.

From that moment in time human nature took a shift, and weak became the new strong, death the new life, and down the new up.

YOUR WEAKNESS
(OR WHAT MAN CAN'T DO)

Have you ever tried to be strong and failed? Have you found that your desire to obey God and to live in righteousness is strong but your ability is lacking? How many times have you said, "I won't do that," referring to some sin in your life, and then went and did it? Weakness often controls you. You know what you want to do, but you just can't seem to do it. Die young? Sure, that sounds good, but practically speaking, not so sure. The feeling of weakness against sin isn't unique to you; it's a part of everyone's walk of faith. In his letter to the Romans Paul displayed his own weakness when he said these words: *"I do not understand my own actions. For I do not do what I want, but I do the very thing I hate"* (Rom. 7:15). How many times have we surprised ourselves with our utter weakness, being completely unable to do what we so desperately want to do and doing what we so desperately don't want to do? Too many to count.

As new believers we all are passionate about obedience. When we first believe we think we can do it all; our passion is so strong. But after a time we start to learn that passion doesn't equal strength, and our sinful nature rears its ugly head. Over time many of us then just give up trying; failure seems so imminent that we say things like, "Well, no one's perfect," and "There's always forgiveness." And we live a defeated life, struggling with sin, sometimes overcoming but mostly losing. It can be a horrible feeling, your own weakness, your own

HERE LIES
MICHAEL

When I was in my teens and early twenties, all I wanted was to be married. And so I got married as quickly as I could to whoever would have me. But I soon discovered that marriage wasn't the answer to all my problems. Instead of marriage being my salvation like I thought it would be, it only further exposed my self-centeredness and brokenness. After only two years of struggle, marriage counseling, and mutual deep hurt, divorce seemed the only option. By year three, my dreams were dashed and the marriage was in the dumpster. Looking back now, I can honestly say that if I had died to myself and lived for God instead, the divorce probably would never have happened. Yet in God's mercy, ten years later I married Hayley. I am certain that God's best is always found in turning over your weaknesses to his strength, and knowing that, in that, you can do all things. If I had known then what I know now, I would have had the gospel-given strength and wisdom to honor my covenant of marriage and the ability to overcome what on my own strength I could not, one sinner living with another sinner. It's through God's grace that Hayley and I are living that out today.

wretchedness, but it isn't meant to be the end of hope but the end of you, and that comes when you surrender the idea that you can do it all in your own strength. The life that embraces its own weakness agrees with the words of God in Zechariah 4:6 that say, *"Not by might, nor by power, but by my Spirit, says the LORD of hosts."*

We attempt to work out so much of our faith by our own power and in our own strength. Even in the lives of the apostles it was the same story. Look at the life of Peter while Jesus walked the earth with him. He was so passionate, so devoted, so certain of his own faith that it appears as though much of what he did was done in that strength of will. But every effort done in his own strength failed. Walking on water ended in going under. When Jesus foretold his betrayal and crucifixion, Peter, with all his strength, rejected it and met with these words from his Savior, *"Get behind me, Satan! You are a hindrance to me. For you are not setting your mind on the things of God, but on the things of man"* (Matt. 16:23). At that point in his faith **Peter could not fully fathom the strength of weakness.** In his mind, weakness was not an option. In fact, when the high priest came to arrest Jesus, Peter believed that in his strength he could defend the Son of God, so he cut off the ear of the servant who was there, only to be reprimanded by Jesus. Wrong again, Peter! And in the ultimate attempt at passionate strength of will, Peter argued with Jesus who said, *"Truly, I tell you, this very night, before the rooster crows, you will deny me three times"* (Matt. 26:34). To this Peter replied with what must have been ardent disagreement, *"Even if I must die with you, I will not deny you!"* (v. 35). **So certain was he**

HERE LIES
HAYLEY

By the time I hit my twenties, I was certain of one thing, that I wasn't good enough or powerful enough to obey God's Word. I had tried all my life to be "good," but my good wasn't good enough for God. And so I had decided by the age of twenty-seven to give up hope of salvation. I had given it my best and my best wasn't good enough, and so I said to a friend, "I've tried to please God, but I'm just not good enough, so I figure since I'm going to hell anyway, I might as well have fun on the way." And so I lived my life of faith in God as one whose faith was only in my sinfulness, not in his goodness. But once God revealed the true nature of himself to me, of his grace given to even the worst of sinners, I was able to say that it wasn't about me anymore, my strength, my devotion, or my ability, but all about him, and his strength, his devotion, and his ability. When my salvation no longer rested on my weak shoulders, I received the strength of God to do the things I was never able to do before.

of his own strength of conviction that Peter rejected the very words of God.

And Peter was not alone; the end of that verse goes on to tell us that the rest of the disciples said the same thing. *"We are not afraid to die!"* was the cry of their strength. But as history reveals, all of these men fell away, running in fear from the fallout of Christ's arrest and crucifixion. Their strength was the weakness keeping them from the passionate conviction they'd felt just hours earlier.

Paul's words ring true for all of us who fail to do what we insist we can do, *"For I know that nothing good dwells in me, that is, in my flesh. For I have the desire to do what is right, but not the ability to carry it out"* (Rom. 7:18). How true it is. But thankfully there is an answer to our weakness that Paul comes to understand and speaks of in his letter to the Philippians. As our faith grows and we come to know more about the attributes of God and his role in our lives and our obedience, we learn to see our weakness in light of these words: *"For it is God who works in you, both to will and to work for his good pleasure"* (Phil. 2:13). And this is where weakness turns into strength, where we go from feeble self-driven soul to strong Spirit-led believer. This is when we understand that we can't sustain faith, prayer, devotion, or obedience for long without the power of the Holy Spirit living within us, teaching us, strengthening us, and setting us free from the power of sin that has for so long controlled us.

It all comes down to surrender. Are you willing to surrender your will to his? Your life to his? And your strength to his? If you are, then instead of fearing weakness you can now embrace it. In his book *Absolute Surrender*, Andrew Murray explains surrender this way:

> *I have a pen in my pocket, and that pen is absolutely surrendered to the one work of writing. That pen must be absolutely surrendered to my hand if I am to write properly with it. If another holds it partly, I cannot write properly. . . . Do you expect that in your immortal being, in the divine nature that you have received by regeneration, God can work His work, every day and every hour, unless you are entirely given up to Him? God cannot.*[7]

The life that is gripped by little gods refuses to die to self and surrender all to God; it is unable to experience the full daily work of God. But the life that fearlessly accepts the "weakness" of surrender finds everything needed for life given by the Giver of life himself.

If you are ready to surrender yourself fully to Christ, to embrace your weakness, and acknowledge that his strength is all you need, then may these words of *Absolute Surrender* be the words of your heart; *"It is impossible for me, my God. Let there be an end of the flesh and all its powers, an end of self, and let it be my glory to be helpless."*[8]

GOD'S STRENGTH

The amazing thing about the acceptance of our weakness and the surrender of our wills is that *"the things which are impossible with men are possible with God"* (Luke 18:27 KJV). If you haven't done a thorough study of the attributes of God, then may we recommend that you do so. When you understand who God is, you can see beyond a shadow of a doubt why your weakness is nothing to be feared, because it just leaves more room for him and his strength. And one of the attributes of God that the entire Christian life is founded on is his omnipotence. The birth of Jesus, his resurrection, everything essential for your salvation was an act of God's power, not yours. As Paul reminds readers in Galatians 2:2–3, *"Did you receive the Spirit by works of the law or by hearing with faith? Are you so foolish? Having begun by the Spirit, are you now being perfected by the flesh?"* Being perfected by the flesh is us attempting to be good and obedient through our own strength.

The Old Testament is full of the lives of men and women who learned about the strength of God by experience. It didn't all come at once. It can take time to fully grasp the strength and ability of the Perfect One, as completely inhuman it is. And so the life of Abraham serves as a shining example to all of us of the power of faith in the One who can. In Genesis 17:1, God called Abraham to be the father of the line from which Christ would be born. This is when he proclaimed his strength, his Almightiness, to Abraham. And from that point on, Abraham learned to trust this omnipotence and embrace his own weakness. He did this first when he was told to go somewhere without knowing where somewhere was (Gen. 12:1–2). Then he was told that he would have a son in his old age, but having to wait some twenty-five years for that son to be born didn't weaken his resolve that though he was weak and old, God could and would still do what he had promised. This plays out in front of us in Romans 4:20–22, where it tells us that no distrust made him waver concerning the promise of God, but he grew strong in his faith as he gave glory to God, fully convinced that God was able to do what he had promised. That is why his faith was *"counted to him as righteousness."* Your human weakness proves God's strength. **There is no danger in being weak where God is strong.** In fact, Scriptures confirm that when you are weak, he is strong (2 Cor. 12:10).

If there is any weakness in your life, don't be shocked; it only affirms that you can't but that God can. If you think that you can do most of the heavy lifting and God can come along and help, you then you haven't fully understood your weakness. You can't do any of it—trusting, obeying, believing, praying;—it all requires God's strength. Look at the lives of the great men and women of the Old Testament. See how all that they did, the great works, the parting of the seas, the surviving in the desert, the crumbling of city walls—all of it—was done through God's omnipotence, not man's strength.

And of course the men and women of the New Testament show so vividly how they could do nothing on their own strength. But when they realized their weakness and only offered their obedience, then they changed a world. Embrace your weakness and God's commands that publicize your weakness and learn to die young.

WHAT IS WEAKNESS?

In the Christian life, unlike in the world around us, weakness, not strength, is a valuable commodity. We have access to the throne of God, not because of our brute strength or steady determination to obey every minute detail of the law, but because of the confession of our inability to do any of it on our own. It is through weakness that we first utter the words, "Dear God, save me." When we come face-to-face with our own weakness and inability to save ourselves, to help ourselves, and to heal ourselves, we are ready to accept the salvation that comes from faith in Christ. We've met so many people on our journey of life who, through hitting the bottom in life, through losing everything, were able to find more than they had ever imagined. Women who were beaten, abused, and left for dead by men who claimed to love them have found themselves with nothing left but a Savior who reaches down to help them when no one else can. Men who have lost everything through addiction, only upon hitting bottom, have been able to see the God of the Bible come alive to them when everything else was dead, including their own hearts.

After hitting just such a bottom, Michael found the faithfulness of God come to life in a jail cell in Washington. "There was nothing left for me but four walls, a toilet, a bed, and a small brown Bible. As I looked down at that book I said, 'Really? Really, that's what this is all about? You're trying to get me back?'" And that's exactly what happened. In that cliché moment, God got him back. And he got him back, in large part, due to his weakness. In the moment when everything is stripped away, when the pit seems like it can't get any deeper, when all you love is lost, then can you truly see heaven reaching down to grab your hand and pull you up. For others, it's not losing anything at all, but rather gaining all the earthly strength possible before realizing it's not enough, that no amount of money, fame, power, or influence can fill that empty void inside. In that moment, too, the illusion of strength and worth is melted away and through weakness God can enter in. And hence, the most radical conversions happen in jail cells and homeless shelters, in mansions and limos.

Weakness, therefore, is man accepting a less than flattering role in his own salvation and worth. It is man being fearless in his inability to change or to save himself and completely confident that his lowly position is far less significant than any place his pride would take him. And so what looks like weakness to the outside world is really the strength of faith to believe God is who he says he is, that his Word is all-sufficient and all that is necessary for righteousness, training, and every good work that God would have us do (2 Tim. 3:16–17).

THE WEAKNESS THAT LEADS TO DEATH

There are many things about faith that seem dangerous to the unfaithful. Aspects of trusting and obeying God make the godly look weak and pitiful to the untrained eye. Even for the believer many of these things might seem inconsistent with life and happiness. But make no mistake; the life that dies to self is the life that lives for God even when humiliation will be the outcome. So let's take a look at some of these weak moments that take the life out of a man so that Christ might enter in.

WAITING IS WEAKNESS

Everyone knows that waiting by the phone for someone you hope will call shows way too much of your weakness for that person. It shows a depth of devotion that reveals your adoration or need for that person and your eager anticipation to hear from him or her, if only across the airways. And that's why even if you wait as you say, "Ring. Ring! RING!" you still act like you were not waiting when the phone finally rings. Waiting on someone is too embarrassing to be shared.

Waiting can also be uncomfortable. Waiting in line is not acceptable to the rich and powerful, who are ushered to the front of the line and given instant access because of who they are. Waiting is seen by many as weakness. But God looks on it with favor. In fact, its reward is, ironically, strength. It says in Isaiah 40:31 those *"who wait for the LORD shall renew their strength."* **As you come to accept the things you can't do, you learn to rely on the One who can.** And it is through prayer that reliance finds its start. As you turn to the One who promises to give you all that you ask (Luke 11:9–13), you learn that waiting on him isn't weakness but strength, as all of your power was never enough to do what God can do in the blink of an eye should he desire it.

Ultimately, it is through continually acknowledging your own weakness, your own inability, and your own absolute poverty that you find the need for complete dependence on God, which shows itself in the waiting. **When you become so certain of your need for him that each moment you look to receive all that you require from him, then waiting becomes the highlight of your day, the source of all your hope.** You must understand how much God wants to give you of himself, his power, and his love and how much he wants to care for your life with all its weaknesses. When you understand this you will wonder why you ever had a problem waiting on God for all that you need, not only for salvation for eternity, but for salvation from sin and for every other need in your life. **God always giving and working, you always waiting and receiving—this is the perfect life.**

Your waiting is weakness turned to strength as you learn not only the character of God but also the way to obedience. In the words of Oswald Chambers, "To wait is not to sit with folded hands, but to learn to do what we are told."[9] **Waiting strengthens the one who waits.**

A great man of faith and prayer, E. M. Bounds, wrote on the subject of waiting on God saying that "faith gathers strength by waiting and praying. Patience has its perfect work in the school of delay. In some instances, delay is of the very essence of the prayer."[10] **God's delay leads to your waiting, so why fear delay that is the very choice of the One you love?** Would he not choose for you only what is best? The truth is that *"a person cannot receive even one thing unless it is given him from heaven"* (John 3:27), not even delay. Allow the waiting to do its work and live for God and not yourself.

TURNING THE OTHER CHEEK
IS WEAKNESS

"Do not resist the one who is evil. But if anyone slaps you on the right cheek, turn to him the other also" (Matt. 5:39). This has got to be another one of the most unwelcomed and misunderstood sayings of Christ. Surely he couldn't mean it literally or completely. There are times when standing up for yourself is necessary—when arguing, fighting back, or resisting are essential to life. Our hearts seem to confirm it. Turning the other cheek is unsafe and leaves us open for all kinds of attack and harm. So why did Jesus say these words? Why would he want us to resist fighting back or at the very least standing up for ourselves? It makes no sense to the flesh. But God has a plan for the weakness that turning the other cheek displays. Jesus never commanded anything that was to be

discarded or left, but all was for our good, to be obeyed and followed in order that we might know and love him more (John 14:21).

Jesus is our perfect example of turning the other cheek. In 1 Peter 2:21–23 we are called to this same turning when we read,

> For to this you have been called, because Christ also suffered for you, leaving you an example, so that you might follow in his steps. He committed no sin, neither was deceit found in his mouth. When he was reviled, he did not revile in return; when he suffered, he did not threaten, but continued entrusting himself to him who judges justly.

Christ's turning of the other cheek reveals itself as weakness becoming strength, because this weakness in the eyes of man is really trust in the One who judges justly. And in that there is ultimate power. As Peter writes in 2:20, *"What credit is it if, when you sin and are beaten for it, you endure? But if when you do good and suffer for it you endure, this is a gracious thing in the sight of God."* Turning the other cheek, enduring suffering when you don't deserve it, and knowing that it's not fair is a gracious thing in the sight of God. It is us showing the evidence of God's grace in our lives to others who would torture and hurt us as they did Christ.

Can you, like Christ, leave mistakes and injustices in your life for God to correct and make right? Can you trust that he will have the final word and that he will work all things out together for the good of those who love him

(Rom. 8:28)? If you can, then your weakness will be your strength, and his graciousness will be yours as well.

SERVING IS WEAKNESS

Jesus came not to be served but to serve. And this idea threw a wrench in the works for the Jews who believed he would come in power and righteous anger. The servant Jesus was not what the religious world expected. Many believe that serving is reserved for the poor, the lower class, the bottom rung. People who serve are often treated as less important than those they serve. Important people serve no one, or so the world believes. But serving is meant for the strong in the way of faith.

The servant isn't concerned with self but with the master. This of course is the most unselfish position one could take. And it's also one of the ways that we allow death to ourselves. As Paul says in 2 Corinthians 4:5, *"For what we proclaim is not ourselves, but Jesus Christ as Lord, with ourselves as your servants for Jesus' sake."* For the world, serving can be seen as weakness, but for the believer it is to follow in the steps of the Savior who *"came not to be served but to serve, and to give his life as a ransom for many"* (Matt. 20:28).

MEEKNESS IS WEAKNESS

Meekness is another one of those ugly biblical words that are so out of style in the modern world. The meek are weak, they are mousy, they are poor, and they are unremarkable. The meek fade into the background, get used and abused, and lose in the battle of life—or so we've come to believe. How many of us clamor to be considered meek in our relationships to others? How many of us pray for the meekness to refuse to fight for ourselves, to be self-obsessed, or to need to be heard? Chances are few to none! Meekness is a weakness that is hard to muster. But this so-called weakness is a description of the life of our Savior (2 Cor. 10:1), and it is meant to be a description of our lives as well. *"Put on then, as God's chosen ones, holy and beloved, compassionate hearts, kindness, humility, meekness, and patience"* (Col. 3:12). What a list!

Meekness is the very essence of a life that knows it can do nothing on its own, except that God allow it or provide it. How many times did Jesus explain his meekness in this way? *"Truly, truly, I say to you, the Son can do nothing of his own accord, but only what he sees the Father doing"* (John 5:19). *"I do nothing on my own authority, but speak just as the Father taught me"* (John 8:28). **Christ's meekness was his resigning himself, in all his power and strength, to the Father, that he might work through him.** It is important here to point out that Christ's meekness didn't come out of his lack of power, since we believe he was, after all, 100 percent God while simultaneously 100 percent man. Our meekness, like that of Christ, should come out of our knowledge of the power and holiness of our Heavenly Father, and from our humility toward God along with our kindness toward our fellow man. So what the world considers weakness, we see as our strength, and that is our meekness.

WEAKNESS LEADS TO DEATH

The man who doesn't know the love of God often goes kicking and screaming to his grave. The idea of death (the ultimate weakness) repulses him, scares him silly, and so death and anything like it is despised by natural man. But

HERE LIES
MICHAEL

I don't know what it is, but nine times out of ten, when I go out to eat, the server gets my order wrong. And you know how much I love food, but because I have been in their shoes, working in restaurants to pay my way through school, I have to overcome my worship of food and instead replace that with a concern for man. While I want to complain and run the server ragged, in respect and love, I consider the servers more important than me, and not the other way around. So I eat what I'm given and accept the table they've chosen. I ask very few questions and request very few additional items like lemons, extra mayonnaise, or a more rare steak. The funny/sad thing is, at home I am a taskmaster to Hayley, far more demanding than I am to some stranger at IHOP. Lord, help me reek of meekness!

for the one who believes in God and the resurrection of the dead to life in heaven, death is a welcomed thing. And so it is with the little deaths of life, those weak moments when we die to self and refuse to serve our own end, no matter the cost. This idea of selflessness, of the importance of God's will over man's, has been seen in the lives of countless men and women who have risen above the rest to serve in ways that can't be imagined by the unrepentant.

One such believer who dared to die young was Josef Tson, an evangelical dissident in Communist Romania. When faced with threats of death by the Ploiesti, Josef replied, "Your supreme weapon is killing. My supreme weapon is dying." See, Tson was a preacher and his sermons had been recorded and sent out to his followers. "If you kill me," he said, "those sermons will be sprinkled with my blood. Everyone will know I died for my preaching. And everyone who has a tape will pick it up and say, 'I'd better listen again to what this man preached, because he really meant it; he sealed it with his life.' So, sir, my sermons will speak ten times louder than before. I will actually rejoice in this supreme victory if you kill me." And at that instant, his weakness, death, became his strength, and the officers sent him home.[11]

When considering what the world calls weakness, check with God. Does he agree, or is he calling it strength? Know your weaknesses, and know where real strength comes from, and trust that it is no great weakness to die young.

CHAPTER 5

SLAVERY
IS THE NEW
FREEDOM

You have been set free from sin and have become slaves of God.
ROMANS 6:22

Real freedom is not the external freedom to gratify every appetite; it's the internal freedom not to be enslaved by our appetites.
JOHN ORTBERG

We've talked about a lot of ugly words—words the world hates and wants nothing to do with, but *slave* takes the cake in the prize for ugly. No one likes the idea of being someone else's slave. Freedom is all-important in the life of man. Freedom means you are free to come and go as you please. You can make your own way, do your own thing. Freedom means never having to be told what to do or when to do it. And so the world covets its freedom and tends to look down on anyone who voluntarily chooses to obey another person and become a servant. The word *obedience* is tied closely to slavery. And both terms give the idea of someone who has given up thinking for him- or herself, or at least is no longer allowed to. And freedom of thought as well as action feels right to man; therefore slavery is unacceptable in any form.

But what the world doesn't know is something that the philosopher/musician Bob Dylan did know, and that is that we all have to serve somebody and that even birds are chained to the sky.[12] **When a man demands the freedom to make his own choices, to do whatever he pleases and to be subject to no one, he deceives himself into thinking that freedom is a possibility.** But in another weird upside-down twist, **the man devoted to freedom**

becomes a slave to whatever freedom he enjoys. In other words, his freedom leads him into another kind of slavery—a slavery to his own passions, rights, and desires. As it says in 2 Peter 2:19, *"Whatever overcomes a person, to that he is enslaved."* And each person who serves freedom will be overcome by that which their freedom allows.

Just take for example the person who wants to be free to experiment with any kind of drug, having no restrictions on what can be done with his or her own body, and see how quickly this freedom becomes bondage—how the body, instead of choosing the drug, requires it, and how that bondage leads to a slavery that is almost impossible to break. That's an extreme case, so how about something less insidious. What about the person who wants the freedom to love whoever completes him or her? This person wants to go after love with a passion and marries the "perfect" person because of the feeling that comes from that person. Then after a few years of marriage it's discovered that those feelings are no longer the same. And since feelings must be obeyed, this person leaves his or her one-time love in search of the next *real* great love. And the story starts all over again, and again, and again, and the happiness that is so looked for never comes.

We can easily see how the lives of people devoted to their own freedom, instead of being free from suffering and pain, become filled with suffering at the hands of their own choices. In James 1:14 this idea is explained as temptation: *"But each person is tempted when he is lured and enticed by his own desire."* So we are tempted by what we want—by our desire to do what we want, when we want it, and how we want. *"Then desire when it has conceived gives birth to sin, and sin when it is fully grown brings forth death"* (James 1:15). So notice the process taken by those who believe they are free to do whatever they want to do. They are tempted by some choice they consider themselves free to make, and then once they give in to that "freedom," they sin. And the result of this sin is death—and not a death to self, but a spiritual death, the kind of death that leads to separation from God and bondage to sin. Second Peter 2:19 calls it a slavery to corruption that comes with a promise of freedom.

So this idea of freedom at the hands of self is really slavery to our passions and emotions, slavery to self. This is where we get flipped; **the freedom we take for ourselves turns out to be slavery**—slavery to our passions, to our addictions, to pleasing man, to being perfect, to having fun, or to being free. So the question is, **is there really such a thing as freedom?** Or is freedom an illusion? A lie of the world meant to tempt us to reject God in favor of self? Is anyone truly free? Or is Bob Dylan right?

The answer is yes, many can be free, but not the people who choose freedom but the people who choose slavery—they are the free ones. In another unbelievable twist, slavery is the new freedom. But it's not a slavery to the base things of this world and to our nature, and not a slavery to man. It's not a slavery to self, to our whims and wills, but to a far greater will. This is a kind of slavery to righteousness, goodness, and love. And it is the kind of slavery that results in your freedom. In 1 Corinthians Paul reminds his readers of their ownership, *"Do you not* *know that your body is a temple of the Holy Spirit within you, whom you have from God? You are not your own, for you were bought with a price"* (6:19–20). This price was the blood of Jesus, spilled to take away your sins that you might be free—not free to sin some more but free to serve God with your life. **The believer is no longer his own, so to demand freedom is to demand to be set free from God,** free to be your own god or to find another that serves you better. This ends up being no freedom at all.

The thing every believer needs to know is *"for freedom Christ has set us free"* (Gal. 5:1), free from any chains that would enslave us and keep us from experiencing the full blessing of God. **To reject the freedom of Christ for the freedom of the world is to submit yourself again to the yoke of slavery.** But those of us who fully accept the love of Christ find this idea at work: *"The love of Christ controls us"* (2 Cor. 5:14). This control is beautiful because it is what allows us to be victorious over sin, to overcome our suffering and pain, and to live life to the fullest.

Many people, in an attempt to be free, have run away from God, claiming that he demands too much of them, that to obey his Word is a slavery they cannot handle, because he is a brutal taskmaster. They fall into the arms of what they consider to be freedom—the freedom to obey nothing but their own emotions, thoughts, and desires. Rather than being told what to do by a God or a book of law, they decide to respond to life themselves, choosing whatever feels good or makes sense to them at the time. These people would have us believe that obeying Christ and living to please him is bondage, slavery to yet another master; but the truth is that **the world** enslaves everyone who hasn't turned their lives over to Jesus.

TO FREEDOM FROM SLAVERY

Slavery is the new freedom because slavery to God gives those of us who embrace it freedom from all other gods, which express their hold on us in the form of struggles, addictions, fears, worries, and all other sins in our lives. But then you have to ask again, *Who is free?* Don't we all struggle with sin? Isn't it a fact that there is no one righteous, not even one? How can we be truly free when sin rules in our bodies? The answer to that is twofold. First, we are free from the condemnation that sin brings on the sinner. After Paul talks about his inability to control himself and to do what he wants to do in Romans 7, he comes to the end of himself and his own strength and quickly asks the question, *"Wretched man that I am! Who will deliver me from this body of death?"* (Rom. 7:24). His answer is the answer for all of us. Its importance is paramount in the life of faith and the foundation of all our freedom. And the answer is: *"Thanks be to God through Jesus Christ our Lord!"* (Rom. 7:25). Jesus is the deliverer of freedom from this body of death. He is the answer to our freedom from the punishment of sin. And here it is, **here is the single-most critical verse in the life of the sinner:** *"There is therefore now no condemnation for those who are in Christ Jesus"* (Rom. 8:1). This is the message of the gospel for a sinful world. And **this is the freedom that slavery brings, freedom from the condemnation that ought to come from sin but doesn't because of the blood of Jesus.** When we realize the depths of our wretchedness and our inability to save ourselves, we get to the end of ourselves, and then and only then we are able to say thank you for the gift of Jesus Christ our Lord. Then we are so able to put out our hands that used to be bound in slavery to sin and offer them up as slaves to righteousness.

But you ask, "How can that be done? How can I be free from slavery to sin so that I might serve God and find the freedom he promises?" We're just like Paul. We do what we don't want to do all of the time. And isn't that the case? We, who ought to live a victorious and free life, live like slaves to the sin that used to control us. That is because we haven't fully understood our freedom. Many of us understand the freedom from the penalty for sin. We understand that Jesus came to set the sinners free from that, but we fail to understand the second truth about freedom which is that he came to utterly put an end to sin's control over the lives of the redeemed. Now, before you start to shake your head in disagreement, let's be clear on this: the one who says, "I just can't be good on my own, I've tried and I've failed. So why hold me to such a high standard?" is essentially using this notion of weakness and inability to obey as a cushion for sin. He or she is saying that obedience, doing what God asks of us, is too hard and so "thank God for grace." While we should be thanking God for the grace that forgives, we should also be thanking him for *the grace that sets us free.*

As long as we all consider sin to be a struggle that we can never fully win, we will continue to lose. Those who struggle fight to keep their heads above water, like a man lost in the middle of the ocean treading water; those who struggle put all their efforts into just keeping afloat. They consider the great expanse of the ocean of sin that they are in, and they say, "I just can't do it. I can't get to the dry land of freedom. It's an impossibility." So they tread water as they struggle with sin, always arguing with it, giving in to it, running from it, and falling back into its arms again. Struggle is then not an appropriate response to sin. In other words, if there is anything in your life that you call a struggle, be it the struggle with worry or fear, doubt or anger, whatever it is that is a major part of your personality and daily life, you would be far better off to call it a sin and to be done with it.

How does calling your struggle a sin make that struggle go away? That's the question that finds its answer in slavery. Take a look at your freedom verse. This is the most essential piece of Scripture for the one who would be done with his or her slavery to sin, the kind of sin that you've never before been able to break in your own power. It's in Romans 6, and it holds the key to your freedom. Let's take a look first at verse 2 where Paul asks the question, *"How can we who died to sin still live in it?"* This is the question we just asked. How can we be dead to sin yet continue sinning? What are we missing? The answer comes in verses 3–4, where Paul goes on to say, *"Do you not know that all of us who have been baptized into Christ Jesus were baptized into his death? We were buried therefore with him by baptism into death, in order that, just as Christ was raised from the dead by the glory of the Father, we too might walk in newness of life."* This is the death we talked about in chapter 1—this death that we died to sin, that we died with Christ, that is death to all that is self. Verse 6 tells us what this death means, and here is where we find the freedom we are talking about.

"We know that our old self was crucified with him in order that the body of sin might be brought to nothing, so that we would no longer be enslaved to sin." What good was the crucifixion then? Was it just for our salvation, for our entrance into heaven? Or does this verse suggest more? Yes, it does, much more. According to this verse, this death took away the power of sin on the lives of believers so that we would no longer be enslaved to sin. How is that possible? And how did we miss that? This is the answer we've been looking for, the way out of the struggle and the defeat. Victory over sin isn't a fantasy but a promise.

The reason we can say that is here in verse 7—sin can no longer control you, or fight with you, and you no longer need to struggle against it because the *"one who has died has been set free from sin."* **This is freedom not just from the wages of sin, but also from the control of sin.** Why? Because *"the death he died he died to sin, once for all, but the life he lives he lives to God. So you also must consider yourselves dead to sin and alive to God in Christ Jesus"* (Rom. 6:10–11). Once a slave to sin, now you are a slave to God. As we read on further in chapter 6, verse 22, *"Now that you have been set free from sin and have become slaves of God, the fruit you get leads to sanctification and its end, eternal life."* So **the fruit of your slavery is freedom from sin, sanctification, and eternal life.**

The image is this: Before your salvation, you were enslaved to sin. You came into the relationship with big chains wrapped around your wrists and ankles, sealed with enormous locks, keeping you from your freedom. But when Jesus set you free from sin on the day he saved you, the lock was opened and the chains were loosened. The trouble is that you didn't know that. So **you've been walking around with chains of sin on your body that only require you to pull your arms apart to enjoy the freedom from the heaviness.** All the pain, all the struggle, all the battles can be ended as soon as you accept the notion that those chains have been broken, and sin is no longer holding the key to the lock.

The only man who is truly free is one who not only believes that slavery to God is what is best for him, but who trusts his master enough to believe that he made arrangements for his complete freedom and not a partial freedom. You cannot be a part-time slave. You cannot serve two masters (see Matt. 6:24). When you serve God as a bondservant, you have the power and freedom to say no once and for all to the sin that controls you. And here is the command to that end, *"Let not sin therefore reign in your mortal body, to make you obey its passions. Do not present your members to sin as instruments for unrighteousness, but present yourselves to God as those who have been brought from death to life, and your members to God as instruments for righteousness. For sin will have no dominion over you, since you are not under law but under grace."* (Rom. 6:12–14) And there it is. Sin has no dominion or control over the one who has exchanged death with life. God's grace assures it.

This should be good news to everyone who believes. If it's not for you, if you feel defeated because you've been so defeated for so long, and if now you're blaming yourself and wondering why you've been living so long in the dark—you have to stop. This is not an opportunity to condemn yourself. We've already established that you are too sinful and too weak to save yourself. And that, thankfully, there is no condemnation for you who are in Christ. So take that to heart. And know that your continual sin, your addictions, your habits that you have been unable to control, these are the things that enslaved you in the past but now enslave you no more, if you are only willing to surrender yourself and to believe that to be a slave to God is to be free from sin. The kind of sin we are talking about here is the enslaving kind, the habitual kind, the kind talked about in 1 John 3:8–9, where it says, *"Whoever makes a practice of sinning is of the devil, for the devil has been sinning from the beginning. The reason the Son of God appeared was to destroy the works of the devil. No one born of God makes a practice of sinning, for God's seed abides in him, and he cannot keep on sinning because he has been born of God."* Here John agrees with Paul. **The practice of sinning is inconsistent with slavery to God because sin is slavery to someone or something other than God**, and you cannot serve two masters. Consistent, habitual sin has its end in your freedom. And that freedom is available to all who will confess their own wretchedness and trust his righteousness.

THE LIFE OF A SLAVE

So what does this life of servitude to God look like? How do we die young to our need to manage our own lives and make up our own minds. It is, after all, man's nature to think of himself? Self is something that God has given every one of us. It is the very center of our being. And the reason he gave us this self was to serve as a container for his life that would come into us. God gave man and only man, not the sun or the moon or the stars or the animals, this self so that every day we can say, "I give you myself, all that I am, to you and your service."

This self that we all have can either be an empty vessel ready to accept the life of Christ into it, a temple to his holy Spirit, or it can be occupied with more human things—self-will, self-effort, self-dependence, self-esteem, self-importance. All of these focus on the little god inside of us rather than the true God above us. But slavery empties itself of all its self-will and determines to please God and to crucify self. The life that doesn't die to self denies the master, refusing to entrust itself as slave, and thereby misses out on freedom.

In his book *Slave of Christ,* Murray Harris defines slavery as this: "The idea, of total dependence, the forfeiture of autonomy and the sense of belonging wholly to another."[13] This definition is frightening when thought of in respect to a human master, but in respect to our heavenly and perfect Master, this definition is the essence of freedom. Why would we not want to be totally dependent on the all-powerful, all-knowing, always present, merciful, gracious, and kind God who is love himself? And why would we want to maintain any kind of autonomy from him when he is the answer to all of our needs, wants, hopes, and dreams? When you think about who it is you are enslaved to, your slavery takes on a whole new meaning.

The characteristics of the slave are seen through different eyes as well. **The slave, in every instance must practice submission, unconditional obedience, and self-denial**. None of those come natural to man. So let's take a look and see how those disciplines draw us into the slavery that leads to freedom.

SUBMISSION

Submission is probably one of the most disdained words in the area of human relationships. The idea of submitting ourselves to someone else to be told what to do and when to do it is downright ugly for most of us. In fact, when we got married and were faced with the whole submissive wife idea found in Ephesians 5:22, the battle was on. Asking a thirty-something, successful, intelligent woman to suddenly become submissive to any man was a counter-cultural concept that had both of us reeling in pain. Michael had no previous experience in leading a strong woman, and Hayley had no love of the word submission. And so it goes for people across the globe who struggle turning their lives over to another to guide and care for.

Sometimes the best way to understand a term is to look at its opposite. So let's try that with submission. **The opposite of submission is defiance. Defiance is open resistance.** As believers we choose between submission and defiance. If I am called to submit to you and you tell me to sit down, I have two options: I can sit and submit or I can stand and defy. In the modern way of relating, submission has been rejected by most in favor of democracy, equality, and shared responsibility. But submission is an essential part of the Christian life for everyone, men and women, both today and tomorrow, for the strong and the weak, the rich and the poor. First, in James 4:7 we are commanded to *"submit [ourselves] therefore to God,"* and second, in 1 Peter 2:13, to *"be subject for the Lord's sake to every human institution."* Then in Ephesians 5:21 we are called to *"[submit] to one another out of reverence for Christ,"* and finally, in Ephesians 5:22, wives are called to submit to their husbands. So submission covers our relationship with God, human institutions (such as police, governments, school, etc.), and one another. **Submission matters to God in all of our relationships.**

But you might be asking right now, why does submission matter to God? Why does he command such a difficult task for his children? There are several reasons, and one is that **our submission to God and to others proves our faith in God's sovereignty.** The wife can fully submit to her husband because of her submission to God. And because of this submission, she promises to serve God and obey all of his commands, of which submission in marriage is one. She also trusts that God can and will speak to her husband and give him the wisdom to lead her as Christ led the church. And if not, then she trusts God enough to know that even then submission is not rejected but serves to prove her faithfulness to the One in whose hand are both the saved and the unsaved. In 1 Peter 3:1–2 we see this principle explained in the command to wives with unbelieving husbands. *"Wives, be subject to your own husbands, so that even if some do not obey the word, they may be won without a word by the conduct of their wives, when they see your respectful and pure conduct."*

Likewise, husbands submitting their very lives for their wives as Christ did for the church is radically un-self-interested. The reason submission makes sense to the believer who trusts God's sovereignty is revealed in the words of Romans 13:1, which command submission to every governing authority; but it's the *why* that really matters here, so let's take a look. **"Let every person be subject to the governing authorities. For there is no** authority except from God, and those that exist have been instituted by God." This speaks to God's sovereignty over all, even those we are called to submit to who may not be smart, kind, or lovable.

Another reason Scripture gives for the call to submission is found in 1 Peter 2:15 where it says that *"this is the will of God, that by doing good you should put to silence the ignorance of foolish people."* So our **submission proves God right and scoffers wrong**. It proves what a large part of the world doubts, and that is that God is good enough to believe and kind enough to submit to. And it proves that when he says he will set us free from the bondage of sin, he isn't lying. **The believer who refuses to submit to God, then, calls God a liar—determining that submission is too risky to the life of self within us**, and therefore has to be rejected as on out-of-date concept reserved for a people from a more socially rigid time.

The great fear that we humans have of submission is of what it does to our self-life, how it takes our self-life and empties it out so that it might be filled by the one we submit to. This concept is counterintuitive to our need for survival. It threatens our very core, our self, and because of that we cringe at it. But precisely because of that cringing and the sensation of death that it brings, God demands it in our lives. When it says in James 4:7 to *"submit yourselves therefore to God,"* it uses the word *therefore* to refer back to something already said. In this instance the *therefore* sends us back to James 4:6, which says these deadly words, *"God opposes the proud, but gives grace to the humble."* Remember that? It all comes back to death, the death that comes through humility.

Submission is the ultimate step of humility; it is calling yourself nothing that the "other" might be something. It is refusing to be the sun and seeing yourself as the planet that orbits it. It is embracing the idea of taking the worst seat, the last place in line, and trusting God to make the last first and the worst the best. The humility that God so wants for his children requires submission. Even Christ knew this. The humility he expressed throughout his time here on earth echoed his submission to the Father. *"I can do nothing on my own. As I hear, I judge, and my judgment is just, because I seek not my own will but the will of him who sent me"* (John 5:30). **Submission reveals our humility while defiance reveals our pride.**

Submission also allows the submissive to practice endurance, a very valuable and important trait in the life of faith. In 1 Peter 2:19 it tells us of unjust submission: *"This is a gracious thing, when, mindful of God, one endures sorrows while suffering unjustly."* Submission is seen in the area of love in these words in 1 Corinthians 13:7, describing love itself: *"Love bears all things, believes all things, hopes all things, endures all things."* The love that doesn't submit never has to endure or bear all the things that love was meant to bear but defies submission in favor of self-exaltation, self-determination, or independence.

In the life of faith, there should be no question as to whether the believer should submit; the only question now is, how does one submit? Or what does submission look like? The best answer to this in every instance is death. Submission looks and feels like death to the one who submits. This death is the death to self that is so often hard to achieve because it threatens our very existence. But submission requires it.

Submission often requires disagreement. It's not full submission to be told, "Go over there and eat that delicious pie." We were going to do that anyway! But **submission is seen when we do what we don't want to do; we do it because we've been told to do it, and our will is killed so that another's will becomes our impetus for acting**. Doing something you don't want to do goes against the grain of our humanity of self, especially when it's at the command of someone else. But for the believer, this state of "slavery" actually produces freedom because it is no longer our will we are fighting for, or defending, but the sovereign will of God that we seek to serve. In this position of submission our obedience becomes our freedom as we replace our sinful and fallen will with the will of our perfect and holy God.

Submission is paying to others that which we owe them. There's another nasty word, *owe*; what could we possibly owe to another? And whose big idea is this anyway? In Romans 13:7 Paul lays out of few of our debts, *"Pay to all what is owed to them: taxes to whom taxes are owed, revenue to whom revenue is owed, respect to whom respect is owed, honor to whom honor is owed."*

Submission is a form of unconditional obedience. That means there are no rules tied to submission, such as "I'll do what you ask as long as it makes sense to me." **Submission doesn't have room for making deals. It simply does what it is told**. And a failure to do what you are told is disobedience and defiance. Of obedience to God, Jesus says this: *"If anyone loves me, he will keep my word, and my Father will love him, and we will come to* *him and make our home with him"* (John 14:23). Of obedience to parents, Ephesians 6:1–3 says, *"Children, obey your parents in the Lord, for this is right. 'Honor your father and mother' (this is the first commandment with a promise), 'that it may go well with you and that you may live long in the land.'"* And of pastors, Hebrews 13:17 says, *"Obey your leaders and submit to them, for they are keeping watch over your souls, as those who will have to give an account. Let them do this with joy and not with groaning, for that would be of no advantage to you."*

The only submission, then, that is unacceptable is submission to sin. Therefore, if anyone commands you to sin, then submission is off the table; to submit to the command to sin would be to sin. In this way, God protects us from dangerous submission both from spouses and authorities. Submission that is inconsistent with God's Word is dangerous and deadly and must be avoided. But submission that is inconsistent with our "rules," ideals, and hopes is not meant to be dangerous to our physical life but to our self-life. In these instances, when submission threatens the very core of yourself, calling you to die to self, to give in to others' desires that rage against your own, it's usually for your benefit and the benefit of the kingdom.

Submission serves an important purpose in our lives because it requires a death that comes from refusing your own will for the sake of another. Submission takes the life out of self and replaces it with Christ. It is a deliberate choice to serve God over self that is manifest in the thoughts and actions of the believer.

HERE LIES
HAYLEY

Submission is one of the hardest and most amazing acts I've ever committed. It promised to rip my life away from me and offer it up as a slave to One who would guide not only my choices but also my actions and my future. I simultaneously hated it and loved it as it revealed to me my preoccupation with self and my need to die young. My desire to obey God's Word on all counts led me to the tough decision to choose submission, not only to my husband, but more importantly to God, to authorities, and to other believers. And in this conscious choice to resist my need to be in control of all, I found freedom from so many of my emotional chains. I found that to die was easier when it accompanied my commitment to surrender my will and submit to the authority of God's Word once and for all. It was as though submission was the shovel that dug the hole and buried me in Christ, because only through submission was I able to say, "Not my will, but yours be done." Submission proved to myself and my God that I believed those words and would live for them as I would die for them.

DIE YOUNG TO BE SET FREE

Jim Elliot, the missionary who gave his life for Christ on the mission field and was killed by the people he went to save, is often quoted as having said this about slavery to God, "God always gives His best to those who leave the choice with Him."[14] There is great freedom in slavery when it is slavery to all that is good and holy. This kind of ownership never destroys, never damages, and never disappoints. It is true that in life you are going to serve somebody; there is no way around it. Our human nature confirms it. You can see it in every inch of the world around you; the question is, whom will you serve? And to what end? Serve yourself and for a while you may find freedom, but it is only an illusion and will not be sustained. Self is ultimately powerless to save or rescue you from the pain and suffering of this world, and ultimately a brutal bondage is the result. When you submit yourself to the ownership of God, you set yourself free to live not by your own strength but by his, and in his perfect and wise will you find everything that you need for life and happiness. It is true that the birds of the air have no freedom from their nature; they are chained to the sky, but because of this complete and total submission to what God made them to be, they have no concern for their lives. As Jesus said in Matthew 6:26, *Look at the birds of the air: they neither sow nor reap nor gather into barns, and yet your heavenly Father feeds them.* When you, like the birds of the air, the lilies of the fields, and the animals of the forests, can trust God with not only your heart, but also with your self, you can be set free from all of the sins that used to entangle you—all your worry, fear, insecurity, doubt, anger, bitterness, resentment—all of it. Freedom is yours when you submit yourself to the only slavery that you were ever meant to be under.

CHAPTER 6

CONFESSION
IS THE NEW
INNOCENCE

*Christ can and will save a man who has been dishonest,
but He cannot save him while he is dishonest.*

A. W. TOZER

*Unconfessed sin is unforgiven sin,
and unforgiven sin is the darkest,
foulest thing on this sin-cursed earth.*

D. L. MOODY

Confession is the act of admitting you were wrong, and no one likes the feeling this brings. In fact, men have died, countries have gone to war, and marriages have been destroyed because of the human aversion to admitting our own error and sin. The act of confessing is humiliating. It threatens self, exposing it to the one who hears the confession, and makes agreement with the "enemy" that the unfavorable ideas about us are actually true. This tears at the very walls of self, threatening to shake it to the foundation. How many times have you seen a politician avoid confession for fear of losing a position, or a parent resist confession for fear of looking weak in a child's eyes? Even a peer will refuse a confession out of the fear of appearing to be other peers. The resistance to confession promises to protect us, to keep up the charade, to help us maintain our power and our image. Confession is a dangerous thing to a life built on the goodness, rightness, and excellence of self.

Without confession of guilt there is no innocence for the sinner. That means confession is a requirement for us all. Confessing precedes forgiveness. First John 1:9 clearly states that *"if we confess our sins, he is faithful and just to forgive us our sins and to cleanse us from all unrighteousness."* The two things go together. **Confession**

precedes forgiveness, just as our first confession precedes our salvation. As it says in Romans 10:10, *"For with the heart one believes and is justified, and with the mouth one confesses and is saved."* So our confession leads to our salvation. Confession is of ultimate importance in the life of faith. In fact, without it there is *no* faith. Only those who fail to confess their sin miss out on the grace and forgiveness of God.

Our resistance to confession does two things: it keeps us from the forgiveness our sins need, and it also calls God a liar because to fail to confess is to say "I have not sinned." And *"if we say we have not sinned, we make him [God] a liar, and his word is not in us"* (1 John 1:10). He says, *"All have sinned and fall short of the glory of God"* (Rom. 3:23). If this is the case, then how is confession not a daily part of our lives, from sunup to sundown? Surely if our sin requires confession, then each day must have its own time of confession.

But confession isn't much talked about in the modern church, meaning the body of believers, beyond the confession of salvation and confession of crimes prosecutable in a court of law. Why do you suppose that is? What is our fear in the area of confession? Could it be all that it requires of man? Of the confessor it requires certain humility, embarrassment, and shame, especially when sin is confessed to or in the presence of another human being. The pain of failure and shame can be overwhelming. Just getting the words out can feel like death. So is it any wonder that we all avoid the act of confession as much as we do?

THE ANATOMY OF CONFESSION

What is confession, exactly? Is it simply saying, "I'm sorry"? **Confession of the biblical sort is the act of verbalizing not only error and remorse but also truth.** When we confess our sin we admit that we were wrong and that God was right. We admit our weakness and his strength, and we admit that we agree with God.

Confession isn't a general statement like, "I'm sorry I was a jerk," or "I'm sorry if I hurt you." Confession gets specific. Thomas Watson puts this idea more poetically when he says, "A child of God will confess sin in particular; an unsound Christian will confess sin by wholesale—he will acknowledge that he is a sinner in general." So **proper confession calls out the sins we committed and not just the pain we inflicted.** When we are honest and specific about sin, then we make agreement with God and confession is made.

Confession is best done instantly. Why wouldn't it be? The sooner you can confess, the sooner you find your innocence. As Thomas à Kempis didst say, "Spit out the poison with all speed, hasten to take the remedy, and thou shalt feel thyself better than if thou didst long defer it."[15] **Confession, like submission, is best done immediately.**

In the life of the Christian there are **two kinds of confession**. There is **the confession that we make to God regarding our guilt and need for his forgiveness.** This is the saving kind of confession, the kind that saves us from our guilt and makes us innocent. And then there is **the confession that we make to man regarding our guilt and our need for healing**. In James 5:16 this kind of confession is explained: *"Confess your sins to one another and* *pray for one another, that you may be healed. The prayer of a righteous person has great power as it is working."* So confession both provides for our forgiveness and our healing.

CONFESS TO GOD

First, let's look at the confession we make to God for the forgiveness of our sins. The Bible is filled with God's words about confession and forgiveness. In fact, the entire book exists for this purpose, to provide the sinner the forgiveness through Christ that is needed for eternal life. It's no wonder that confession is talked about so much throughout the Bible.

We've all heard people say that *"if God is all-knowing then why do I need to pray? He already knows what I've done, what I'm thinking, and what I need."* And while his omniscience does mean he knows everything, he still requires the participation of man in the equation. **To leave everything to his omniscience is to remove the responsibility and the necessity for man to participate in his own interior life**. It's the idea that we would be less aware of our sin if we didn't speak it and that we wouldn't participate in the equation without it. God doesn't allow for that; instead he wants man to speak, and by his speech to hear himself agreeing with God and accepting his own guilt, thereby tenderizing his heart to the promptings of the Holy Spirit and the commands of God. In Proverbs 28:13–14, God makes this important statement: *"Whoever conceals his transgressions will not prosper, but he who confesses and forsakes them will obtain mercy. Blessed is the one who fears the LORD always, but whoever hardens his heart will fall into calamity."* Now

who can you conceal your transgressions from that really matters? Certainly you can't conceal them from God. And most of the time they are very evident to man. So **confession reveals your sinfulness and your dire need for God mainly to yourself, and it convinces you of your need for a Savior.** But sinners who remain silent aim to convince themselves through their own silence that they aren't as bad as all that.

And certainly our confession, when heard by man, reveals not only a fellow sinner who understands our own struggles, but God's redeeming power in the life of that sinner. Your confession, when made and then redeemed by the forgiving power of the blood of Jesus, allows onlookers to see God at work and to get firsthand proof that he does heal our diseases and take away our sins (Ps. 103:3).

Another beauty of confession is the power that gets behind it. 1 John 2:1–2 reveals that when you confess, you don't do it alone, but Christ confesses with you as an advocate for you and your forgiveness. We are promised that *"if anyone does sin, we have an advocate with the Father, Jesus Christ the righteous. He is the propitiation for our sins, and not for ours only but also for the sins of the whole world."* So our confession is not done alone or in our own strength, but with the power of Christ himself.

Confession leads to peace. There is nothing more nagging than our feelings of guilt. Guilt can haunt. But unconfessed guilt can also lead to turmoil of a more physical kind. Family problems, enemies, interpersonal relationships are greatly strained by the presence of unconfessed sin. In Leviticus 26:40–42 God made a promise to his people with regard to their confession, and this is what he said:

> If they confess their iniquity and the iniquity of their fathers in their treachery that they committed against me, and also in walking contrary to me, so that I walked contrary to them and brought them into the land of their enemies—if then their uncircumcised heart is humbled and they make amends for their iniquity, then I will remember my covenant with Jacob, and I will remember my covenant with Isaac and my covenant with Abraham, and I will remember the land.

And so the turmoil that came out of their iniquity, which was being brought into the land of their enemies, will come to an end. Peace comes on the wings of confession.

God wants your confession; he wants you to acknowledge your guilt and in the words of Hosea 5:15 to earnestly seek his face. Confession breeds earnestness. It reminds us not only of our rejection of God, but also of our need for him and his amazing grace.

God's grace takes away the guilt of man in exchange for the innocence of Christ. It's his exchanging his death for our life, and our willingness to offer up our death for the life that he lives in us. Those who *die young* confess this truth eagerly, "I am nothing and you are everything." This confession repeats the words of Ephesians 2:8–9 and allows us to breathe a sigh of relief. *"For by grace you have been saved through faith. And this is not your own doing; it is the gift of God, not a result of works, so that no one may boast."* In this kind of economy of faith, confession is the new innocence because of the grace that rewards it.

CONFESS TO MAN

Now let's look at the confession we make to man that leads to healing. Isn't it interesting that God provides confession not only as an avenue for the protection of our humility, but also as an avenue for healing? And this healing isn't only the healing of physical and emotional pain, but of spiritual pain as well. God's best exists for the believers in community in relationship to one another (Gen. 2:18). Community is a part of who God is as seen in the Trinity. So **life for believers is best lived in community**, and one of the blessings of community is the gift of confession and prayer that we can share with one another. As we confess our sins to each other, we share God's forgiveness with each other in a tangible, audible, maybe even tactile way that reminds our souls how true it is. God allows for our need for human interaction and assurance that God is who he says he is, and that forgiveness is available for all, in spite of what the world might say about our sinfulness.

But in our failure to confess to one another, many of us retreat to the comfort of confessing to a God we cannot see. As much as we don't like admitting we were wrong, it is somehow easier to say that to God than to man. Many times our confessions to God might be more statements we make to ourselves about being better next time and thankfulness that God is forgiving. They might never get to the heart of a confession that states the sin and accepts the responsibility for it. But in the presence of another human being we are less likely to be unsure of our confession. As we confess to another we are forced to come face-to-face with the ugliness of our sin and to voice our guilt as a semipublic testimony of our imperfectness and his perfect trustworthiness.

On the heels of confession comes the prayer of those believers who heard it. They are standing in the gap, praying for our healing from the crippling pain of sin and its effects on our bodies. Not that all suffering is caused by sin in our lives, but God promises to relieve our suffering as we confess our sin. It might not be the sin that we confess that caused our pain, but our feelings about the pain, our resentment, bitterness, unforgiveness, worry, or doubt need confession. No matter the case, **confession of our sins and the transparency and authenticity that it brings is healthy for the soul and for the community.** Your confession allows another person not only to have insight into their own sin but also to have the grace of God on that sin as well.

As a believer you have two avenues of confession. Both are invaluable in the life of faith and both serve different purposes. But when is confession called for? Under what promptings and what circumstances do you need to confess? "When I am guilty," you answer. And you would be right, but maybe only part of the time. So let's take a look to see when guilt should be confessed and when it should be rejected.

CONFESSION OF GUILT

Confession is oftentimes misunderstood because of our relationship with guilt. Guilt is something almost every human being feels; with the exception of perhaps the sociopath or the psychopath, all of us will live with moments or even years of guilty feelings and the pain that comes from them. That's owing to our inborn sense of right and wrong and the judgment that accompanies it. But **the feelings of guilt you experience are not always proof positive of your guilt**. That's because there are **two kinds of guilt** in this world—there is **godly guilt,** or grief, **and worldly guilt,** or grief. Both claim your sinfulness, but not both are accurate. And the difference is this: *"Godly grief produces a repentance that leads to salvation without regret, whereas worldly grief produces death. For see what earnestness this godly grief has produced in you, but also what eagerness to clear yourselves, what indignation, what fear, what longing, what zeal, what punishment!"* (2 Cor. 7:10–11). This means there's good guilt and there's bad guilt. **Guilt can be associated with actual sin, or guilt can be associated with regret, pride, or a misunderstanding of God's Word.** In the former case, you are guilty of dishonoring God, while in the latter, you are only guilty of focusing on yourself.

First let's take a look at the godly guilt or grief that we see in 2 Corinthians. **The cause of godly guilt is always sin.** And when you are willing to accept the pangs of this guilt as a red flag revealing the sinful areas in your life, this will lead you to repentance. **Repentance is your changing your ways, determining what sin is in your life and how to avoid it from here on out.** Godly guilt comes from doing things that Scripture forbids— anything from disobeying authority to complaining about discipline, being angry with God (Isa. 45:24), not being a good listener (Prov. 18:13), always thinking about yourself (Phil. 2:3–4), being proud (Prov. 29:23), lying (Prov.13:5), and coveting (Col. 3:5), to doubt (Rom. 14:23), worry (Matt.

6:25), and fear (Isa. 44:8). The list could go on and on, but you get the picture. **When you feel guilty after doing any of the things God forbids, then confession is your only exit.**

Godly guilt leads you to God, not to self. And out of that comes your awareness of your utter sinfulness and your need for a perfect Savior. In this moment there is a death to the sin in you that held so tightly to your soul. And this death comes from your confession of the true nature of your sin.

But worldly guilt is something altogether different, and any discussion of confession and innocence has to include talk about this worldly guilt. In our book *Over It*, we said worldly guilt happens *"when the guilt you are feeling is misplaced, when it is guilt not over sin but over failure, suffering, mistakes, embarrassment or a missed opportunity."*[16] Godly guilt was meant to convict you of sin against God, not against man or self. So worldly guilt misses the mark, and therefore worldly guilt is to be rejected, not confessed. To better explain, here are a few examples of worldly guilt. **When you feel guilty after you've already confessed a sin to God, this is worldly guilt.** The sin you confess to God is forgiven sin, no matter how big it was. To continue to fret about it and hold on to it is to say God isn't big enough to forgive you and your special sin. It is an affront to God and a lie of the biggest kind that comes from the prince of lies, the accuser from the garden.

Feeling guilty because you missed out on something, messed up, or failed is feeling the sting of worldly guilt. Missing out, messing up, or failing (unless it's failing to do what God asks you to do) is not sin, and there-

fore the feelings of guilt are untrue. Also, feeling guilty for doing what God loves but what man hates is not godly guilt. There may be hurt feelings involved, but there is no guilt associated with obedience. In Luke 14:26–27 Jesus says, *"If anyone comes to me and does not hate his own father and mother and wife and children and brothers and sisters, yes, and even his own life, he cannot be my disciple. Whoever does not bear his own cross and come after me cannot be my disciple."* So **there is no guilt in loving God over man**.

Godly grief or guilt leads to godly sorrow, and this is a good thing that leads to confession and repentance. The believer need not hold on to any feelings of guilt. As soon as guilt convicts of sin, confession is called for. But if the guilt you feel doesn't point to sin in your life, then that guilt can be discarded as useless and built around pleasing man, not God. Guilt's job is to convict us of sin and then lead us to repentance, not to remain as a lifelong stowaway in our hearts.

Because worldly guilt can haunt your life and leave you feeling condemnation where there is none, you must have an understanding of what constitutes guilt and what doesn't. There is no reason to be ruled by feelings of guilt when Christ came to remove your guilt. And this we know from the words of 1 Timothy 1:15, which confirm that *"Christ Jesus came into the world to save sinners."*

ACCEPTING CONFESSION

Everyone wants forgiveness for themselves; our guilt demands it, and God easily and quickly gives it. But he also allows and even expects a process by which one man hears another man's confession in order to bear one another's burdens. We see this in Colossians 3:13–14, which says to *"[Bear] with one another and, if one has a complaint against another, [to forgive] each other; as the Lord has forgiven you, so you also must forgive. And above all these put on love, which binds everything together in perfect harmony."* But hearing the confession of another requires a great deal of death on the part of the man who hears it. There are two kinds of confession that you will hear from the people around you. The first is a confession of a sin that has nothing to do with you. The second is the confession of a sin that affects you deeply. In the first instance the danger in hearing the confession is our human tendency toward judgment. As Jesus points out, *"You judge according to the flesh"* (John 8:15). That means we judge based on self, how it makes us feel, what *we* think of the sin. And in this, our tendency is to look down on the sins of others all the while completely ignoring that our own are just as bad or worse. Of this Jesus says,

> Judge not, that you be not judged. For with the judgment you pronounce you will be judged, and with the measure you use it will be measured to you. Why do you see the speck that is in your brother's eye, but do not notice the log that is in your own eye? Or how can you say to your brother, "Let me take the speck out of your eye," when there is the log in your own eye? You hypocrite, first take the log out of your own eye, and then you will see clearly to take the speck out of your brother's eye. (Matt. 7:1–5)

Hearing another's confession is not a time to work on the speck in that person's eye, but a time to speak God's truth and forgiveness back to the confessor. We must resist the flesh that wants us to be judgmental and decide instead to be unfazed by the confession that he or she, like you and me, is an imperfect person prone to sin and in dire need of forgiveness.

So according to Romans 15:1, "*We who are strong have an obligation to bear with the failings of the weak, and not to please ourselves.*" This means that we have to listen without shock or despair and in many cases, when the person is in our care, such as a child or a student, without taking the sin as an indictment on us. **The hearing of a confession should never be about us, but about God, whom the sin offended.** It should be a chance to remind the sinner of God's gracious gift of forgiveness (Eph. 2:4–7). In doing this we become a living Bible to those whom we love and whose confession we hear.

The second type of confession you will hear is the kind you hear from someone who has hurt you deeply, maybe even repeatedly. This kind of confession is probably the hardest to hear. After all, it requires not only your speaking of God's forgiveness but also of your own. In the back of all our heads is the notion that to offer our forgiveness to them is to justify the person, to release the confessor from the guilt and thereby to release him or her from the consequences of the injustice. And this the human heart cannot stand. Jerry Bridges describes the flesh's distaste for forgiveness with these words, "**Forgiving costs us our sense of justice.** We all have this innate sense deep within our souls, but it has been perverted by our selfish sinful natures. We want to see 'justice' done, but the justice we envision satisfies our own interests. We must realize that justice *has* been done. God is the only rightful administrator of justice in all of creation, and His justice has been satisfied. In order to forgive our brother, we must be satisfied with God's justice and forego the satisfaction of our own."[17]

From this position our **forgiveness is our giving up our right to hurt another in retaliation for hurting us.** It's our giving up the role of "sinned against," and allowing sin to be what it is—a rejection of God and not of us, a refusal to obey God's will instead of our own. When Nathan confronted David on his transgression, David was beside himself with anguish. These words he spoke can teach us the right way of thinking about sin. In 2 Samuel 12:13, we read the words that David said when confronted with the sin of his taking Bathsheba and killing her husband: *"I have sinned against the LORD."* But he had taken a woman who wasn't his and killed her husband; surely his sin was against these two human beings. Yet David puts his confession of sin at the rightful place; sin is a rejection of God's commands and so must be taken to God, judged by God, and avenged by God if vengeance is required. **Taking the role of God onto yourself by refusing forgiveness or seeking revenge is turning others' sin into your own.** And what's more, it's making your requirements for forgiveness greater than God's. After all, if God can forgive any sin but blasphemy against the Holy Spirit (Mark 3:28–29), then your requirements for forgiveness are more stringent than his. This means that you consider yourself more righteous than God. And that can't be the case, so **your forgiveness admits that you do not require more of man than God**

does. It accepts God's judgment as the only judgment that is necessary.

Forgiveness is a requirement on the life of the believer (Matt. 6:15; 18:21–35; Col. 3:13). And whether it feels dangerous, weak, or unfair, it has to be done; your very forgiveness rests on it. Matthew 6:14–15 says this of forgiveness: *"For if you forgive others their trespasses, your heavenly Father will also forgive you, but if you do not forgive others their trespasses, neither will your Father forgive your trespasses."*

Forgiveness, both heavenly and earthly, requires only one thing. Luke 17:3 reveals what that is: *"If your brother sins, rebuke him, and if he repents, forgive him."* **Repentance precedes forgiveness.** If you are having a hard time forgiving someone who has sinned and not repented, then this verse should set you free. Repentance makes forgiveness possible, both from God (Acts 3:19) and man. So a wife wouldn't forgive an abusive husband for the hits that he continues to be proud of by saying, "I forgive you honey," because that is offering forgiveness where it isn't due (Matt. 18:18). Still, when we are hurt by others who fail to repent, we have to swallow our pride and our self-interest and allow ourselves to let go of our hatred, bitterness, resentment, and other sins that have come out of their sin. **The ability to get over abuse, hatred, even murder, and to get on with love and even service to our enemies (Matt. 5:44) is repugnant to man, but required by God.** When we refuse to let another person's sin be an excuse for our own, we allow grace the upper hand on sin. Then we will be able to say with Joseph, *"As for you, you meant evil against me, but God*

meant it for good" (Gen. 50:20), and there is the strength for us all, found in God's sovereignty and power.

Confession is a requirement in the life of faith, and so is forgiveness. We must never forget to what great depths we have been forgiven. And out of that we must learn to *"be kind to one another, tenderhearted, forgiving one another, as God in Christ forgave"* us (Eph. 4:32). Allow forgiveness to be a natural part of your relationship with others, and it will be a natural part of God's relationship with you. After all, *"If you do not forgive others their trespasses, neither will your Father forgive your trespasses"* (Matt. 6:15). And this no soul can bear.

CONFESSION LEADS TO DEATH

Sin is ugly and an embarrassing thing to reveal in ourselves. It shows the depths of our imperfection and wretchedness, and being honest about it can bring on the pangs of death. All of us want to be viewed for our goodness—the places where we get it right and not where we get it wrong. But this notion that we are never wrong or mistaken is deceitful and destructive. **To refuse to be honest about our sin is to refuse to agree with God that there has never been and will never be a perfect person besides Jesus.**

Confession leads to death because confession kills the sinful part of your life that used to lay claim to it. Confession buries your sin with Christ and removes it as far as the east is from the west (Ps. 103:12). It is through confession that we can identify ourselves with the death of Christ and let him put to death the things of this world.

Confession reveals not only our sinfulness but God's righteousness. Refusing to confess our sins to

HERE LIES
MICHAEL

I have a confession to make. I'm currently obsessed with confession. I'm obsessed with how we create families and church communities where confession is an anomaly or even discouraged. I don't have any easy answers on how to create a culture of confession in your family or church other than to start living transparently and confessing before you're found out. That's why the majority of our sidebars in this book are confessional; they destroy pride in us, create healing, and maybe even encourage the same action/reaction in you. Confession lets the confessor and the hearer (or reader) know that they're not alone, both in the pursuit of healing and the dismantling of a double life.

those we love is refusing to allow them to see the hand of God at work in our lives. **Confession is good for the soul and bad for sin.** In fact, sin cannot stand confession. It turns the lights on, exposes it, and cleans things up. Confession is essential in the life of faith, and without it our innocence is suspect.

Our failure to confess makes us all liars (1 John 1:8). While the fear of confession promises us that to confess is to be exposed and vulnerable, the truth is that to confess is to stand in agreement with God. So **the way to innocence is by admitting guilt.** Wow! And there you have another upside-down moment. God came to save not the righteous, but sinners, to give sinners their righteousness while those who believe they are righteous because of how good they are become forever guilty.

When you die young you are honest about sin because you care less about your own life and standing than you do about God and his standing. There is in all of us the knowledge that no one is perfect; so where we fail to see confession we see hypocrisy, and where we see hypocrisy we are unimpressed if not turned off al together. In the family of faith confession is essential not only to our forgiveness but also to our relationships. While confession feels like overwhelming guiltiness, it is actually overwhelming innocence.

CHAPTER 7

RED
IS THE NEW
WHITE

*Though your sins are like scarlet, they shall be as white as snow;
though they are red like crimson, they shall become like wool.*
ISAIAH 1:18

*Would you be free from the burden of sin? There's power in the blood,
power in the blood. Would you be free from your passion and pride?
There's power in the blood, power in the blood.*
LEWIS E. JONES, 1899

The color red conjures up a lot of images in the human mind. A woman in red symbolizes seduction. The scarlet letter, assigned to the adulterous woman, was a shade of red. Red flags are meant to be warnings of impending danger. A thief is caught red-handed. Prostitutes live in the red-light district. The character of the Devil is often seen in red. Red is the color of blood and a symbol for guilt, sin, and even anger. It is understood by most that if you drive a red sports car you will be pulled over more times by the police than if you were driving the same car in white. Red gets our attention; it has a sense of danger, sin, and guilt associated with it.

White carries an entirely different sentiment. For centuries brides have worn white as a symbol of purity. White is considered a clean and bright color. Doctors and nurses often wear white. Some cultures view white as a sign of royalty. In early Westerns you could always spot the good guy because he rode a white horse and wore a white hat. A white knight is a man who rescues someone in need. If you were to see two women, one dressed in red and the other in white, you would probably associate innocence with the woman in white and looseness with the woman in red. You would never expect to see a

The Cross of Jesus Christ destroys all pride. We cannot find the Cross of Jesus if we shrink from going to the place where it is to be found, namely, the public death of the sinner. And we refuse to bear the Cross when we are ashamed to take upon ourselves the shameful death of the sinner in confession.

DIETRICH BONHOFFER[18]

RED IS THE NEW WHITE

woman wear red to her wedding; the imagery is just too incongruent.

In the book of Revelation we see continual use of the color white on the people and the creatures that surround God. Revelation 3:5 reveals such an image of Christ in white when it says, *"The one who conquers will be clothed thus in white garments, and I will never blot his name out of the book of life. I will confess his name before my Father and before his angels."* And the book of Daniel shows us a similar scene when it says, *"As I looked, thrones were placed, and the Ancient of Days took his seat; his clothing was white as snow, and the hair of his head like pure wool; his throne was fiery flames; its wheels were burning fire"* (7:9). Revelation 19:14 says, *"And the armies of heaven, arrayed in fine linen, white and pure, were following him on white horses."*

It should be no surprise that the Bible uses the colors of red and white to symbolize both guilt and innocence, death and life. In Isaiah 1:18 God tells us that *"though your sins are like scarlet, they shall be as white as snow; though they are red like crimson, they shall become like wool."* Consider the magnitude of this idea. **Red is a fast color, meaning that it is almost impossible to take red and make it white.** If you've ever stained a white shirt with blood or tomato sauce and tried to get it out, then you know how colorfast red can be. **Red is a stubborn reminder of our mistakes and often refuses to go away.** In Revelation 12:3, red is the color of the dragon and symbolizes the Devil's cruelty. And in Revelation 6:4, the red horse comes to take peace from the earth.

So how is it then that red is the new white—the new innocence and purity? In this ultimate act of turning things upside down, making red white, God takes red, the color of blood, and applies it to our ugliness and sin in order to make us white as snow, justified in his eyes, no longer held guilty of our sin. **As red covers white so well and so permanently, so blood covers the sins of man.** Since the gates to the garden were closed to us, sin has ruled the lives of man, and so blood has flown. The very first time blood flowed on earth was the blood that flowed in order that Adam and Eve might be clothed after their fall (Gen. 3:21). Soon after that, the first act of man worshiping God involved blood. Hebrews 11:4 tells us that *"by faith Abel offered to God a more acceptable sacrifice than Cain."* And the covenant that God made with Noah came after Noah's first sacrifice after the flood, which we see in Genesis 8:20, *"Then Noah built an altar to the LORD and took some of every clean animal and some of every clean bird and offered burnt offerings on the altar."* God's covenant with Abraham required blood. In this act of worship Abraham's own blood was to be shed as a symbol of his commitment to die to himself in the form of the sacrifice of his son Isaac. But as Abraham lifted up the knife to kill his self-life in his son, God made a substitute for that blood with the blood of the ram (Genesis 22). Blood was also used to spare the Israelites from the plague of the death of the firstborn and was to be a signal for the Lord to pass over their homes. And when God confirmed his covenant with Moses, blood was not only sprinkled on the altar but was also thrown onto the people (Exodus 24).

In Hebrews we read about this moment with these important words:

*Not even the first covenant was inaugurated
without blood. For when every commandment
of the law had been declared by Moses to all the
people, he took the blood of calves and goats,
with water and scarlet wool and hyssop, and
sprinkled both the book itself and all the people,
saying, "This is the blood of the covenant that
God commanded for you." And in the same way
he sprinkled with the blood both the tent and all
the vessels used in worship. Indeed, under the
law almost everything is purified with blood,
and without the shedding of blood there is no
forgiveness of sins.* (Heb. 9:18–22)

Leviticus 17:11 tells us why the blood was used as
atonement for God's people when it says, *"For the life of
the flesh is in the blood, and I have given it for you on the
altar to make atonement for your souls, for it is the blood
that makes atonement by the life."* As you look deeper
into God's Word, you will see that blood was needed for
many things. When a house or a priest was consecrated,
when a child was born, when a sin was to be forgiven, at
the times of the festivals, always in everything, in order
to have fellowship with God, blood had to be involved.
**The worshiper never came empty-handed; he always
needed blood in order to worship.** Even the high priest,
who would go inside the veil to the mercy seat once a
year, went into God's presence but *"not without taking
blood"* (Heb. 9:7). The Most Holy Place where God dwells
can only be approached with the blood.

Why all this talk and need for the blood, you might
ask. After all, blood comes only from one place—the
death of a living thing. Must something die in order for

RED IS THE NEW WHITE

163

God to be happy? As we saw in chapter 1, *"The wages of sin is death"* (Rom. 6:23). So according to God's law anyone who sins must die. The idea that God cannot stand the sins of man is a biblical one. Our sins provoke God's anger. This is not an out-of-control, irrational anger, but a holy and righteous anger that is opposed to everything that is evil. His anger toward and opposition to evil can't be glossed over or dismissed as inconsistent with his grace. It is because of **his grace that his opposition doesn't destroy us; but his grace doesn't remove his anger—only the blood can do that**. As we've said, blood requires death, so in the Old Testament God allowed for substitutions to be made. And these substitutions lost their lives in order that the sinner might be forgiven and reconciled with God. And so for the Israelites, the blood seemingly flowed morning and night because of the sinfulness of man and the need for fellowship with a holy God. These blood sacrifices of the old covenant now teach us about the importance of the blood and the need for a sacrifice to be made for sin.

The old covenant prepared us for the coming of Christ and the shedding of the blood of the Lamb, once and for all. In Hebrews 9:11–14 it is written:

> But when Christ appeared as a high priest of the good things that have come, then through the greater and more perfect tent (not made with hands, that is, not of this creation) he entered once for all into the holy places, not by means of the blood of goats and calves but by means of his own blood, thus securing an eternal redemption. For if the blood of goats and bulls, and the sprinkling of defiled persons with the

ashes of a heifer, sanctify for the purification of the flesh, how much more will the blood of Christ, who through the eternal Spirit offered himself without blemish to God, purify our conscience from dead works to serve the living God.

Christ came to be the final sacrifice for man, and his blood is enough to cover us all. His death becomes our life, and his blood our propitiation.

RED IS INNOCENCE

His blood now means our innocence. His blood takes our filth and covers it all, removing all the stains and blemishes and making us white as snow. His red is our new white because as we read in 1 John 1:7, "*The blood of Jesus his Son cleanses us from all sin.*" God cannot accept the sinner; he cannot have fellowship with him or bring him into his presence except for the blood. The blood of Jesus served as the final sacrifice to not only cover our sins but also to remove the punishment for them. In the blood of Jesus is seen all of God's grace. Through the blood Jesus substituted his life for ours as seen in these words in Romans 5:8: "*God shows his love for us in that while we were still sinners, Christ died for us.*" And the atonement, that which repaired the relationship between man and God, was made possible by the blood and by nothing else. **We have to beware the thinking that it was out of God's kindness and love that he saved us. Certainly he is kind and he loves us, but it was out of the death of his Son that he saved us.** We can't rely on God's kindness or love to gain us access to the throne; it is only through accepting the blood that we can be viewed as innocent and allowed entry.

In Matthew 26:27–28 Jesus says to his disciples, *"Drink of it, all of you, for this is my blood of the covenant, which is poured out for many for the forgiveness of sins."* The blood, then, wasn't truly the blood of Jesus. There was nothing magical in the cup; his blood wasn't literally required in the stomachs of the apostles in order for them to be saved but was symbolic blood. The blood that covers our sins is not a literal blood, but a symbol of the death that Jesus died for us. When you bleed you don't necessarily die, but biblically, the "blood" of Jesus represents the death of Jesus. It was his death, as seen in the blood, that secured our release from the penalty of sin. But his death did so much more.

RED IS SALVATION

In sixteenth-century Holland King Philip of Spain controlled the country. When the people revolted, the king sent his army to squelch the revolt. The army went from house to house knocking down doors and killing everyone inside. Inside one particular house, a group of men, women, and children were hiding from the murderers. They were certain of nothing but their terrible deaths. But then a young man had an idea. He took a goat they had in the house, killed it, and then swept the blood under the doorway out into the street as quickly as he could. Then they cowered in silence.

When the soldiers reached the house and started to bang on the door, one of them saw the blood coming out from under the door and shouted, "Come away, the work is already done here. Look at the blood beneath the door." And the people inside the house escaped simply because of the blood.[19] This story is reminiscent of the story of the first Passover. The blood on the doorposts protected the people behind the door. And so it is with the blood of Jesus; his blood ceases God's wrath against us. Romans tells us that *"we have now been justified by his blood, much more shall we be saved by him from the wrath of God"* (Rom. 5:9). But what does it mean to be justified? To justify means to declare as righteous. The blood of Jesus declares that we are now righteous. Acts 13:38–39 can help us better understand what this means. The verses say, *"Let it be known to you therefore, brothers, that through this man forgiveness of sins is proclaimed to you, and by him everyone who believes is freed from everything from which you could not be freed by the law of Moses."* That means you are saved from having to save yourself—saved from being perfect. You're even saved from dying perfectly. The law and all that it might demand cannot ever save you. But through the blood, and that alone, are you forgiven and saved from everything that being good promised to do for you.

Second Corinthians 5:18–21 puts it this way:

All this is from God, who through Christ reconciled us to himself and gave us the ministry of reconciliation; that is, in Christ God was reconciling the world to himself, not counting their trespasses against them, and entrusting to us the message of reconciliation. Therefore, we are ambassadors for Christ, God making his appeal through us. We implore you on behalf of Christ, be reconciled to God. For our sake he made him to be sin who knew no sin, so that in him we might become the righteousness of God.

So because of the blood, God will not count your sins against you but will be reconciled with you and no longer angry or separate. And there is the hope; there is the white knight on the white horse coming to save us all. His blood is making us white as snow.

All of this happens as soon as you believe. It requires no other work than that, as seen in Romans 4:2–5:

> For if Abraham was justified by works, he has something to boast about, but not before God. For what does the Scripture say? 'Abraham believed God, and it was counted to him as righteousness.' Now to the one who works, his wages are not counted as a gift but as his due. And to the one who does not work but believes in him who justifies the ungodly, his faith is counted as righteousness.

But we are aware that to believe something this amazing seemingly requires a great effort on the part of the believer. There is in all of us an idea that this can't possibly be enough, that some work must be done, and so we can easily buck at the concept of justification simply through the gracious gift of Christ's blood. But this is where death becomes you. **You must, in order to receive justification, believe that the blood is enough. You must die to the part of you that insists it do its part to participate in this salvation thing and to help out God.** This part of us that might lie hidden underneath all our talk about gospel or God's grace cannot be left to seduce our hearts. It must die in order that belief can do its work. It was Abraham's faith that was counted to him as righteousness; and the only act Abraham did was believing, which at times, especially at the time of the testing on Mount Moriah, would have been a feeling not unlike natural death. **If your heart has a hard time believing justification by the blood, then consider killing the part of you that would argue against God's gracious and necessary gift.** Without this acceptance there is nothing you can do that can bring you back into right relationship with God.

Justification is God's reaching down to man, not man's reaching up to God. Man sinned, broke God's standard, and became impure. And so man was in need of the righteousness of God in order to get back into right relationship with him. The blood provided this. Ephesians 1:7 agrees, *"In him we have redemption through his blood, the forgiveness of our trespasses, according to the riches of his grace,"* as does Romans 3:22, which confirms, *"The righteousness of God through faith in Jesus Christ for all who believe."*

RED IS PURIFICATION

In his Sermon on the Mount, Jesus tells us who has access to God. His words must have shocked as many when he spoke them as they do today because he says that only the pure in heart shall see God (Matt. 5:8). This means that if you are a child of God then you have a pure heart, even if at times you would object, for his word confirms that those who have access to God are pure in heart. And thanks to the blood you have access to God. Ephesians 2:13–18 should be the victory cry for all who believe:

> But now in Christ Jesus you who once were far off have been brought near by the blood of Christ. For he himself is our peace, who has made us

both one and has broken down in his flesh the dividing wall of hostility by abolishing the law of commandments expressed in ordinances, that he might create in himself one new man in place of the two, so making peace, and might reconcile us both to God in one body through the cross, thereby killing the hostility. And he came and preached peace to you who were far off and peace to those who were near. For through him we both have access in one Spirit to the Father.

Did you get all that? Because of the blood you have been brought near to God; that makes you a part of the "pure in heart."

See, the blood has broken down the dividing wall of hostility between you and God, making peace between you and reconciling you to him. Because of this you now have total access to the Father—access that is only granted to the pure. In the Old Testament, the unclean were not allowed to worship or enter the temple until they were cleansed because the unclean cannot draw near to God. This might sound frightening to you, a sinner. For many of us, the sins of the past continue to haunt us, and we are unable to forget the terrible things we've done. We see Christ and then we look at ourselves and we cringe; how unholy are we, how ugly. But the point of the blood isn't to keep you there; it's to purify you from the stains of your sin, to move you forward. The blood is our bleach.

To belabor your sinfulness is to ignore the blood that cleanses you from all unrighteousness. When we die young we die to our right to hold on to the memory of our sins, holding them tightly in our arms, crying over them, unwilling to let them go because of the sheer magnitude of them all. **The blood not only removes our guilt, but according to Hebrews 10:1–2 it cleanses our consciousness of sins.** The blood holds all the power not just to forgive our sins but also to move us past them, to free us from the pain and suffering associated with reliving them and thinking about them, bemoaning them and belaboring them.

Rather than worry or fret over the magnitude of our sins we, like David, can say, *"Have mercy on me, O God, according to your steadfast love; according to your abundant mercy blot out my transgressions. Wash me thoroughly from my iniquity, and cleanse me from my sin"* (Ps. 51:1–2). And we can be confident that he will do just that.

RED IS VICTORY

I heard an old, old story,
How a Savior came from glory,
How He gave His life on Calvary
To save a wretch like me;
I heard about His groaning,
Of His precious blood's atoning,
Then I repented of my sins
And won the victory.
O victory in Jesus,
My Savior, forever.
He sought me and bought me
With His redeeming blood;
He loved me ere I knew Him
And all my love is due Him,
He plunged me to victory,
Beneath the cleansing flood.

I heard about His healing,

Of His cleansing pow'r revealing.

How He made the lame to walk again

And caused the blind to see;

And then I cried, "Dear Jesus,

Come and heal my broken spirit,"

And somehow Jesus came and bro't

To me the victory.[20]

Your victory has already come. If it doesn't feel like it, don't fret; it's only because you didn't know it was yours for the taking. The book of Revelation shows you your future; just take a look and see what the blood will do: *"And they have conquered him by the blood of the Lamb and by the word of their testimony, for they loved not their lives even unto death"* (Rev. 12:11). It would do all believers good to remind themselves each day of the power of the blood, to bathe in it, to pour it over their mind and their hearts that they might never forget the power in the blood. These words mean so much and offer us the truth that will set us all free.

Red is the new white. And what a beautiful sight it is. Own it. Take it. Enjoy it. You came to him covered in the filth of your sin, ugly, tired, worn out, and wondering what hope you could find. But now that you've been bleached white by the red blood and the power that it holds, you will never be the same. You can't be—his Word confirms it. *"If anyone is in Christ, he is a new creation. The old has passed away; behold, the new has come"* (2 Cor. 5:17).

FINAL LAST WORDS

You are never too old to die young. It is never too late. Too much of your life has not passed. You have not made too many mistakes for God to forgive. But you can make today the turning point in your life—the point when you determine to completely bury yourself in Christ so deep that nothing can ever really harm you again. When you do that, when his love is all that surrounds you and all that contains you and all that you contain, then life is a whole new ball game. What was down is now up, what was death is now life, what was less is now more, and what was weakness is now strength; there is no more death for you. It is all nothing but life. *No one can kill you when you are already dead.*

> *I counted dollars while God counted crosses,*
> *I counted gains while He counted losses,*
> *I counted my worth by the things gained in store*
> *But He sized me up by the scars that I bore.*
> *I coveted honors and sought for degrees,*
> *He wept as He counted the hours on my knees;*
> *I never knew until one day by the grave*
> *How vain are the things that we spend life to save;*
> *I did not yet know until my loved one went above*
> *That richest is he who is rich in God's love.*

—AUTHOR UNKNOWN

ABOUT THE AUTHORS

Hayley DiMarco is the founder of Hungry Planet, where she writes and creates cutting-edge books that connect with the multitasking mind-set. She has written numerous best-selling books for both teens and adults, including *God Girl*, *Mean Girls*, *Idol Girls*, *Dateable*, and the 2007 and 2010 ECPA Christian Book Award winners for youth, *Sexy Girls* and *B4UD8*. She blogs regularly at www.hungryplanet.net, tweets from @hayleydimarco, and disciples young women online at www.godgirl.com.

Michael DiMarco is the publisher at Hungry Planet and oversees cover and interior design as creative director, as well. He has written numerous best-selling books for both teens and adults, including *God Guy*, *Cupidity*, *Unstuff*, *All In*, *Almost Sex*, and the 2010 ECPA Christian Book Award winner for youth, *B4UD8*. He blogs regularly at www.hungryplanet.net, tweets from @dimarco, and ministers to young men at www.godguy.com.

Michael and Hayley live with their daughter on the shores of Old Hickory Lake just outside of Nashville, Tennessee.

SOURCES

1. Robert Morgan, *Nelson's Complete Book of Stories, Illustrations & Quotes for Speakers* (Nashville, TN: Thomas Nelson, 2000), 285.

2. Oswald Chambers, *My Utmost for His Highest: Selections for the Year*, NIV ed. (Westwood, NJ: Barbour, 1993), 306.

3. John Mayer, "Gravity," by John Clayton Mayer, *Try*, Columbia, 2005, compact disc.

4. A. W. Tozer, *The Pursuit of God* (Harrisburg, PA: Christian Publications, 1948), 45.

5. Hayley and Michael DiMarco, *Unstuff: Making Room in Your Life for What Really Matters* (Carol Stream, IL: Tyndale, 2010), 88.

6. Tozer, *The Pursuit of God*, 106.

7. Andrew Murray, *Absolute Surrender* (Chicago, IL: Moody, 1895), 87.

8. Murray, *Absolute Surrender*, 24.

9. Oswald Chambers, *My Utmost for His Highest*, 213.

10. E. M. Bounds, *The Necessity of Prayer*, World Invisible, accessed August 11, 2011, http://www.worldinvisible.com/library/bounds/5bb. 10596-necessity%20of%20prayer/5bb.10596.c.htm.

11. Josef Tson, "Thank You for the Beating," *Christian Herald*, April 1988, 54.

12. Bob Dylan, "Ballad in Plain D," *Another Side of Bob Dylan*, Columbia, 1964.

13. Murray Harris, *Slave of Christ* (Downers Grove, IL: InterVarsity, 2001), 106.

14. Jim Elliot, *Daily Christian Quote*, accessed August 11, 2011, http://dailychristianquote.com/dcgobedience2.html.

15. Thomas à Kempis, *The Imitation of Christ*, trans. William Benham (New York: P. F. Collier, 1909), 366.

16. Hayley and Michael DiMarco, *Over It: Letting God Get You Past Life's Hurts*, (Grand Rapids, MI: Revell, 2011), 95.

17. Jerry Bridges, *The Practice of Godliness*, (Colorado Springs, CO: NavPress, 1983), 207–8.

18. Dietrich Bonhoeffer, *Life Together* (New York: Harper and Row, 1954), 114.

19. Paul Lee Tan, *Encyclopedia of 7700 Illustrations: Signs of the Times* (Garland, TX: Bible Communications, 1996), 340.

20. Eugene Monroe Bartlett, "Victory in Jesus," 1939.

PERSONAL NOTES